DREAM
JOBS
IN
SPORTS
REFEREEING

LARRY GERBER

ROSEN
PUBLISHING®

New York

Published in 2015 by The Rosen Publishing Group, Inc.

29 East 21st Street, New York, NY 10010

Copyright © 2015 by The Rosen Publishing Group, Inc.

First Edition

Library of Congress Cataloging-in-Publication Data

Gerber, Larry, 1946-

Dream jobs in sports refereeing/Larry Gerber. — First edition.

   pages cm. — (Great careers in the sports industry)

Includes bibliographical references and index.

ISBN 978-1-4777-7525-7 (library bound)

1. Sports officiating—Vocational guidance—United States— Juvenile literature. I. Title.

GV735.G47 2015

796.023'73—dc23

2013038834

Manufactured in the United States of America

CPSIA Compliance Information: Batch #S14YA: For further information, contact Rosen Publishing, New York, New York, at 1-800-237-9932.

CONTENTS

INTRODUCTION

Players, coaches, and fans can show their emotions when a game is in the balance. It's the official's job to stay cool and keep the game under control.

It's late in the game, and the championship is on the line. The fans are roaring. The coaches are yelling instructions. The players are exhausted, struggling for that last drop of energy. They have been working toward this moment all season long. Nobody wants to lose.

The final play happens so fast that it shocks everyone! Was that the winning score? Wasn't there a foul? Didn't the player step out of bounds?

For a brief moment, all eyes are on the official. This decision is going to be debated, possibly replayed on video again and again. One side is going to be elated, the other is going to be devastated—even furious! The pressure is on, and this call had better be right!

Although most fans don't stop to think about it, that official may have been practicing for this moment longer than the players,

Being a good official, like being a good player, takes practice. Here, umpire Dan Mickelberg is in position to make a close call during the Little League World Series.

and maybe even longer than the coaches. Whether it's a referee, an umpire, or a linesman, no matter what the sport, no matter the level—from a Little League game to the Super Bowl—it's the officials' job to stay focused when everyone else is losing their cool.

Sports fans know all about their star athletes, but few of them think much about what it takes to be an outstanding official. It's a job that takes preparation, mental toughness, and physical conditioning. Just like players, some officials have more natural talent than others, but no one gets to be really good at it overnight. Reaching the top level of a sport is probably harder for officials than it is for athletes. Those who don't have what it takes—or those who are just unlucky—never make it.

There are lots of places to start. Thousands of games and thousands of jobs are out there for referees and umpires in youth and amateur sports. Some of them are paid, but many aren't. Most umps and refs do their jobs just because they love their sport and want to help people play it.

For most of them it's a part-time job. Sports seasons last only part of the year, and it's hard to make a year-round living by officiating. A few, however, do make it a full-time career, sometimes by officiating in more than one sport.

The major professional and college leagues are always on the lookout for talented officials, but there aren't a lot of openings for those assignments, and competition for them is tough. Scouts from the big leagues look for years of experience and training. They watch games, review film and video of officials in action, and look in at training camps to evaluate candidates. Only the elite make it to the big leagues.

It's not a job for everyone. Officials get little applause. They are constantly criticized. Good officials must also be able to criticize themselves and learn from their mistakes. They need other qualities too—quick judgment, good communication skills, tact, and confidence, just to name a few.

Even the best-known referees and umpires at the top levels of sport say they would rather not be in the spotlight. If you're interested in becoming an official, however, here's a closer look.

Chapter 1
IT'S OFFICIAL

W hat's the difference between a backyard game where everybody's horsing around, and a "real" game that counts for something? The real game will feature regulation equipment and uniforms, of course.

Then there's the playing field. The backyard boundaries might be marked off by trees, rocks, or soda cans. The real field is carefully measured and marked. In the real game, somebody will be keeping score and marking down a win or loss on a team's record.

The real game will likely also have fans in the stands—lots of people who really care about the outcome. For sure, it will have at least one referee or umpire. Official games need officials.

THE "THIRD TEAM"

Ask any sports fan who's watching a game how many teams are playing, and the answer will probably always

Norm Schachter, shown here talking to the Detroit Lions' Alex Karras in a 1965 game, became one of the top officials in the NFL. He emphasized teamwork among officials.

be "two"—if you get an answer at all. From a fan's point of view, it's a silly question.

It's not exactly the right answer, though. Norm Schachter, a senior referee for twenty-two years in the National Football League (NFL), calls officiating crews the third team.

It's true that nobody pays much attention to that third team of officials, except in those brief moments when they're making a call. That's just the way they like it, says Schachter. "We live by the rule 'If they don't know who's working the ball game, you've had a great day,'" he wrote in his book *Close Calls: The Confessions of a NFL Referee.*

Schachter refereed Super Bowl games and NFL championships and later worked for the league evaluating officials and editing the rules. He also wrote the officials' manual for the NFL. He says the more anonymous an official can be, the more likely he is to be successful. However, the attention will come sooner or later. When it does, it probably won't be applause.

Fans usually don't pay attention to the referee or the umpire until it's time to make a call. Then everybody's suddenly focused on the official. However, those brief moments are just a small part of an official's job.

What's the rest of it? Obviously the details are different for every sport. A hockey ref has to be a good skater, and a baseball umpire needs to know the right position for a play at the plate. In general, however there are some things that officials in any sport should try to accomplish.

The National Association of Sports Officials and editors of *Referee* magazine list four main goals for officials. They are keeping the game safe, keeping it fair, helping athletes develop, and promoting sportsmanship.

KEEPING IT SAFE

Enhancing game safety is one of an official's top duties in any sport. It may mean inspecting players' safety equipment and the equipment used in the game. Soccer referees check out the goals and netting; a football official might

Keeping games safe is an important part of an official's job, and that often means enforcing penalties. When players get mad, someone is more likely to get hurt.

look for hazards such as loose turf; and baseball umpires inspect bats to make sure they're regulation.

When the game starts, officials still have player safety on their minds, only decisions must come much faster. Giving first aid isn't part of the job, but referees must decide when to stop play so injured players can get medical attention. They need to know the difference between a hurting player and an injured one.

Most sports also have "flowing blood" rules, so refs watch for signs that a player is bleeding and must leave the game to avoid spreading disease. Contact sports, especially football, have been adopting new rules to prevent concussions. Officials need to keep up with the changes and know what to watch for.

Officials are generally trained not to react to unruly crowds. Crowd control is the job of the league or school game managers. But officials have to do their best to protect players if someone actually charges onto the field or court.

Keeping the game in hand is also a safety issue. When players get mad and lose control, someone is more likely to get hurt or a fight is more likely to break out. Refs need to know when it's time to penalize bad behavior or even eject someone. Penalties are part of keeping the game fair as well as safe. Striving for fairness is another main goal for sports officials.

KEEPING IT FAIR

To ensure fair play, officials obviously must know the rules as well as or better than anyone else on the field. Studying the rule book and keeping up with new rules are the first things recommended for anybody who wants to become an official in any sport.

Mechanics—proper positioning on the field or court and proper use of signals—is another subject that officials must master. They must know the right place to be on every play so they can see and judge the action—and stay out of it themselves.

Sports can be painful, but is the player really injured? Officials often have to make quick judgements about stopping play because of an injury.

To be in the right place at the right time, officials obviously have to be in good physical shape. Hustle and conditioning are just as important for officials as for players.

So is emotional control. Like just about everyone else, officials remember when they've been insulted, bullied, or treated unfairly. An official may feel angry or annoyed with a player, coach, or team who has given him or her a hard time. It takes a special kind of personality to set those feelings aside and be fair when calling the next play or the next game.

That sort of attitude is part of what sports psychologists call "mental toughness." It means being able to work through problems outside the game as well as on the field or court. Family problems and money problems are distractions that happen to everybody, but good officials need to be able to set them aside when the game begins so they can focus on the job.

Officiating usually means a lot of travel. Missed flights, flat tires, lost luggage, wallets stolen from hotel rooms—those have all happened to officials during a busy season. A referee or an umpire who's developed mental toughness will be able to set those worries aside and concentrate on the game. If a referee makes a bad call or loses control of a game, fans and players don't care about his or her personal problems.

It sounds like a lot to ask, but people who love officiating say it's worth it. In a video on the Web site of the National Association of Sports Officials, Mike Pereira, former vice president of officiating for the National Football League, says "It's really rewarding, because you make the game fair."

"I mean, it's really incredible. You always don't make the popular decisions, but you do what you can to establish a level playing field, no matter what sport it is."

HELPING PLAYERS AND PROMOTING SPORTSMANSHIP

Referees and umpires are also there to help players get better, especially at the lower levels of a sport. They're not coaches, of course, and nobody wants them to be. However, in some leagues, especially youth leagues, officials may take extra care to explain rules that apply in certain situations and to encourage players.

Senior officials often conduct preseason clinics for players and coaches, demonstrating such things as what is a foul and what isn't. Basketball referees show players the difference between carrying and legal dribbling or between legal and illegal screens. A baseball umpire may show pitchers what a balk looks like and how to avoid it. Players can then practice the right techniques and improve.

There's more to sports than just winning and losing. Good officials also try to promote good sportsmanship.

During a game, a ref may tell basketball players to watch their feet when lining up for a free throw. It doesn't give anyone an advantage, and it prevents a lane violation that would break the flow of the game. In some leagues, a referee might tell a player that it's OK to run the baseline to inbound the ball after a made basket.

Encouraging sportsmanship is usually always a good thing, once an official learns what's acceptable in his or her league. If a football player helps up an opponent after a clean hit, the referee might give a nod and quietly say "way to go." An umpire might say "good work" to a batter who hands the catcher his mask after it's been tossed aside on a pop-up.

In many leagues, officials also compliment players after a nice play or give quiet encouragement. They need to treat both sides the same way, of course, and not appear to be cheerleaders.

These sorts of instruction and encouragement aren't the main part of an official's duties, and they're practiced more often in some leagues and sports than in others. Officials at all levels help players develop simply by working their games.

WHAT'S THE JOB LIKE?

Veteran officials say the best place to learn the job is to start at the bottom, meaning community recreational leagues, church leagues, and younger kids' games.

Some of these jobs might pay a few dollars per game, but most of them don't. The good news is that there's a place to start learning in every community and there's practically no age limit. Lots of local programs and recreation leagues practically beg for officials, and many of them offer training sessions and clinics that are open to everyone.

There's obviously a lot of difference between a game played by youngsters in the local park and a pro championship in a packed stadium. That doesn't mean the park game is any easier to call.

In baseball and softball, for example, recreational or youth league games may have only one umpire instead of the four that are regulation in upper leagues. The home plate umpire not only has to call balls and strikes but also has to make calls on the bases and down the foul lines.

Because everyone's fairly new to the game, all sorts of unusual and even goofy situations can develop. It makes life interesting for a beginner referee or an umpire, and it's a great way to test your on-field judgment skills. The object, of course, is for everyone to have fun, but the games can still be intense.

The crowds may not be huge at the neighborhood park or gym, but for the fans and players the stakes might seem every bit as high as those of a major championship. Many fans are moms and dads, or brothers and sisters of the players, and the game is a family matter.

Families can take winning and losing very seriously. Some parents put a lot of pressure on their children to perform well. When a call goes against their kid, they may take it personally. That means a lot of emotional pressure for an official.

In "Tips for Youth Sports Officials," the National Youth Sports Officials Association (NYSOA) has several suggestions for referees and umpires. The most important goal, it says, is simply being good at the job—by studying the rules, watching more experienced officials, and practicing to improve, just as the players do. It's important to keep in mind that the game is for the players; officials are there to help them have fun.

Some leagues have officials' manuals that spell out pre-game procedures, but NYSOA recommends that officials in any sport show up at least fifteen minutes before game time to talk with their partners about ground rules and any special concerns, particularly safety issues.

Sometimes it takes courage to do the right thing. Coaches and fans may want to start or continue a game in spite of bad weather or other unsafe playing conditions. It's the officials' job to use common sense and not be intimidated into allowing play if they don't feel that it's safe. If something bad happens, an official might be blamed for letting the game go on.

Youth sports officials shouldn't tolerate rude behavior or cursing from anyone. Young people at this level are playing to learn, and disrespecting officials should be actively discouraged. It's suggested that officials be up front with coaches and let them know that abusive language or behavior will not be tolerated.

Officials also need to be sure they know their league's policies on what to do if fans get out of hand. Sometimes this may mean stopping the game so the proper authorities can deal with the problem.

Focus is important. It may happen that a referee calls a peewee football game with young kids, then later in the day is assigned to a game between older players with

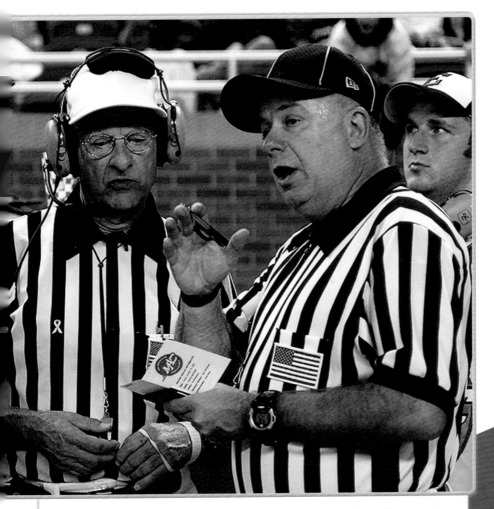

Officials check their rule book during review of a play in a college football game. Rule books are an essential part of officials' equipment at all levels of sport.

better skills. One game may be slow and full of mistakes, the other might move very fast. It's important to concentrate and stay in control.

The association also suggests that youth league officials try to be humble and learn something from every game because there's always room to improve. For good officials, there will be opportunities to take the next step up the ladder—to high school junior varsity and varsity games. Before making the move, think about whether you're ready and whether you really feel comfortable about taking on more demanding jobs.

REFEREEING FROM AN OFFICE

Being a referee means different things in different sports. One of the biggest and most unusual referee jobs is in tennis. Tennis referees are also known as supervisors because their job is to oversee all aspects of a tournament. Fans don't usually see tennis referees on the court unless there's a problem.

Their work starts well before tournament play. The referee takes a list of players and creates a draw sheet, a bracket similar to those used in basketball tournaments. The winners of the first-round matches meet in a second round, and so on.

The referee then schedules the timing of the matches and the courts where they're to be played. He or she then assigns the on-court officials—a chair umpire and lines persons for each match.

Tennis referees usually work in an office behind the scenes. It's the chair umpire's job to make on-court rulings and decide disputes. However when players refuse to abide by the umpire's ruling or when there's an argument about a rule interpretation, the referee may be called to make the final judgment.

Tennis referees are trained and certified by the U.S. Tennis Association (USTA), the International Tennis Federation (ITF), or the Intercollegiate Tennis Association (ITA). They also have to pass an annual test given by a USTA trainer-evaluator to stay up to date on rule changes.

Officials in the USTA start out as provisional umpires. The USTA explains how to get started as a tennis official on its Web site.

Tennis referees have responsibility for just about everything that goes on during a tournament. This discussion between Andy Murray and referee Andrew Jarrett was about closing the stadium roof at Wimbledon.

OFFICIATING SCHOOL SPORTS

Working with a youth league or community sports program is a great way to get officiating experience, and these programs are always looking for volunteers. The jobs don't pay much, if anything, and they usually don't have very strict requirements. For officials in school sports, it's a different story.

Referees and umpires for junior high, junior varsity, and high school games need to be approved by their state's interscholastic association. They may also need to be a member of their local referees' association.

High school officials, like this one in California, have to pass exams on rules and mechanics. In some states, there may also be a probationary period.

High school officials have to pass exams on rules and the mechanics of officiating in their sport, and there are usually certification fees. There's probably an age limit as well. There may be a background check to make sure the applicant doesn't have a criminal record.

In some states, there's a probationary period for new officials. They may be allowed to work only junior high or junior varsity games for a year or two before calling high school games. They will probably need to attend clinics in the off-season to keep up to date on rules and procedures, and they will likely be graded on their performances. Only the best officials are chosen for playoff and championship games.

The good news is that high school officials can count on being paid for their work. Many interscholastic associations post details of their requirements and pay schedules on the Web, and there's a list of state associations at the National Federation of State High School Associations' Web site.

Moving up to a community college or university program means higher pay, but it also takes more time, more commitment, and more travel. It requires several years of high school experience. You'll have to take more exams and probably join another association.

The National Collegiate Athletic Association (NCAA) ranks teams into three divisions according to the size of their schools. New officials start out in Division III or

College officials usually work games among smaller schools before they can get jobs in NCAA Division I. Their work is graded and evaluated along the way.

Division II, working smaller college games, before they can hope for a shot at the major games in Division I. Their work in games will be observed and evaluated every step of the way.

There are more opportunities for women to officiate college sports than ever before. The U.S. Bureau of Labor Statistics (BLS) says most new jobs for referees and umpires will open up in women's college and high school sports.

There aren't many opportunities in the pro leagues. In 2013, there were 121 referees in the National Football League, 70 umpires in Major League Baseball, 61 referees in the National Basketball Association, and 77 referees and linesmen in the National Hockey League. Most of those officials have been doing their jobs for years, even decades, and only a few leave each year.

Across the United States there are about twenty thousand people officially counted as employed sports officials, meaning they get paid for their work. Tens of thousands more are working games without pay and trying to make it a regular job. It isn't easy to make the big leagues.

Chapter 2
STARTING OUT

Many officials come to love their sport by playing it, and they become referees or umpires because they want to stay close to the action. You don't have to be a former player, of course. But ex-players do have some advantages, more so in some sports than others.

For example, practically all hockey referees and linesmen are former players because superior skating is obviously a must, and so is endurance on the ice. There are several line changes during a hockey period, and players get to rest while the game goes on. There are no substitutes for officials, though. Their only rest breaks are between periods.

Former players have become officials in all major sports, and many of them have reached the highest level. Mike Carey was a running back at Santa Clara University in California before making it to the NFL as an official. He was chosen as referee for Super Bowl XLII, becoming the first African American selected for the top assignment in American football. NFL official Chad Brown also played in the league.

There have been many Major League Baseball players who went on to become Major League umpires, although none of them are active today. Only three former National Basketball Association (NBA) players have made it as refs in the NBA, although many of them have been outstanding players in college.

Violet Palmer, the first woman to officiate an NBA game, was a point guard on Division II championship teams at Cal Poly Pomona. She was not only the first

It's not necessary to play a sport before becoming an official, but many officials do. Violet Palmer, an outstanding college player, was the first woman to referee an NBA game.

female NBA ref, but she and Dee Kantner, both hired in 1997, were the first women to reach the top tier of officiating in any major professional U.S. sport. Kantner was a college athlete, too, but not in basketball. She was a field hockey player at the University of Pittsburgh.

Former players officiate at all levels of sport. In some places, former Little Leaguers can become umpires at age thirteen when they're too old to play Little League any more.

Strength, coordination, and conditioning are qualities that can carry over from playing to officiating. Just looking like an athlete can help an official get ahead. NCAA conferences not only want their officials to be in top condition, they want it to look obvious. Coaches, fans, and players are less likely to respect an official who appears to be out of shape.

THE RULE BOOK

Another advantage players have is knowing the rules—at least some of them. That's not good enough to make it as a referee or umpire, however. If you do a Web search for "how do I become an official," you'll see that studying the rule book is one of the first recommendations put out by leagues and experts in any sport.

Officials must know the rules better than anyone else on the field. The easiest way for a ref to lose credibility and respect is failing to know the rules of the game.

"You may never use a rule your entire life, but must be prepared for any situation that comes up," official Tim Holland wrote in his blog post "10 Tips to Becoming a Good High School Football Official." He suggests mastering the rule book by studying one chapter at a time before moving on to the next one.

Officials in Holland's association are given short rules exams each month to prepare them for the major annual rules test administered by the National Federation of High School Officials. Top officials say they spend at least fifteen minutes every day studying their rule books, no matter how many years experience they have.

In youth sports, many leagues have special local rules, which vary slightly from the basic rule book. Rule books at all levels may be hard to understand because they often read like something written by lawyers. The NYSOA suggests speed-reading through the entire rulebook at first, just to get a basic idea of everything that's inside.

Then it suggests putting the rules into categories because some of them are more important to learn early on than others. The NYSOA suggests learning the rules by these categories: 1) the definitions of terms because knowing these will make the rest of the reading easier to understand; 2) live ball and dead ball situations; 3) chapters on various aspects of the game, such as kicking plays in football, pitching in baseball, and out-of-bounds rules; 4) fouls and penalties; and 5) violations and penalties. (Fouls are

Strike two! In addition to knowing the rules, officials study mechanics. That includes the proper use of signals and positioning.

generally infractions involving contact, while violations are infractions of other rules. In basketball, for example, charging is an offensive foul; goaltending is a violation.)

Other suggested categories for study are: 6) chapters that deal with scoring and timing; 7) players and substitutions; 8) officials and their duties; 9) courts, grounds and equipment; and 10) rule changes and points of emphasis.

When studying a rule, it's a good idea to look up related plays in casebooks to get a firm grasp of it. Casebooks contain examples of how rules are applied in game situations. The NYSOA also suggests talking with local rule experts at association meetings and other get-togethers.

For a small fee, Little League umpires can join the Umpire Registry. This entitles them to download rule books and instruction books from the Internet, and it has the latest information on training clinics, seminars, rules updates and interpretations, and videos and other training material. You can check out the Little League's Web site for more information. Organizations in most sports and most levels have similar programs for their officials and people interested in becoming an official.

Another area where officials must study, practice, and be graded is their mechanics. Mechanics include proper use of signals and positioning—what to do and when to do it in every possible game situation. For example, when should a home plate umpire take responsibility for covering a fly ball hit down the third base line? It can be more

LOOKING OUT FOR EACH OTHER

Officials in youth sports are often close to the fans. At high school, college, and pro games, there are more likely to be fences and security personnel to keep rowdy fans from getting out of hand and on to the field or court. Officials at the neighborhood park may not have that sort of protection.

The NYSOA offers these safety tips:

1. Stay with a buddy, another official, or a crewmate. Walk together from the locker room to the car after the game so that if an ugly situation arises, there's someone there to be a peacemaker—or a witness.

2. Be on the lookout for potential problems, especially when there are crowds around. Two pairs of eyes are better than one.

3. Appearance is important. Wear your uniform properly, and look like you belong on the field or the court. An "official" appearance helps win the respect of fans and players.

4. Keep the game moving. Don't skip official procedures, but let the game establish a rhythm and don't interrupt the flow for something that can be handled later.

5. Don't snap back at players or coaches who get angry, vulgar, or profane. It may be hard to resist when someone is in your face, but officials who answer curse words with a tirade of their own usually just make things worse. The solution may be simply to eject the angry coach or player and move on.

complicated than it sounds because some games have crews of two umpires, some have three, and some have four. The correct answer may vary for each size of crew and will depend on the situation. Are there runners on base? Which bases?

Besides studying the officials' manual for your sport, a good way to learn mechanics in amateur and youth leagues is by watching senior officials, asking questions, and hooking up with a mentor.

WORKING WITH PEOPLE

A mentor is a trusted adviser who helps a newcomer learn the skills of his or her trade and may also have good advice on how to get ahead in the profession. Many local officials' associations have regular mentoring programs, where beginners are paired with senior officials. Mentors may help evaluate game performances, help with problem areas, and introduce the newcomer to the officials responsible for game assignments.

When it comes to game assignments, most officials will acknowledge that there are politics involved. It's not just a matter of what you know, it's also who you know. Some officials don't care much for that. They feel that refs and umpires should be judged on their performance rather than on the influential people they know. They might complain in private about associations where "insiders" arrange for themselves and their friends to get the best jobs.

However getting to know people and making a good impression are critical for officials who want to move up in their sport. There's nothing wrong with making sure you're known to the people who decide on hiring and handing out game assignments. It's essential, in fact.

If a sports coordinator has a choice between two officials of roughly equal ability and experience, and if he or she knows and likes one but doesn't know the other, the game assignment is most likely going to the official who's known. It's only human nature.

Meeting the people who can help you get ahead is known in the business world as networking, and a lot of networking goes on in officiating, too. It's important to learn what's OK and what's not when it comes to dealing with those influential people in your area, and this is another way a mentor can help.

It's one thing to be introduced to a conference commissioner, make sure he or she has your résumé, and knows you want to work games in that conference. It's another thing to call the commissioner at home at night to see if you can talk

Umpire Tim Farwig *(right)* talks to his son Augie during a high school baseball game. Mentors can help younger officials learn their trade, on the field and off.

yourself into a job. Trying to get around the regular procedures in order to get ahead usually backfires.

No matter how many people an official knows, he or she is going to be hired or promoted mostly on the basis of character, reputation, experience, and skills. The NYSOA suggests that officials join one or more associations, try to meet as many game assignors as possible, make sure they have your résumé and any other information they need, and be patient.

Also, it can't hurt to learn who's responsible for finding last-minute replacement officials, because emergencies happen. Sometimes scheduled officials can't make it. The person responsible for officials may appreciate a quick phone call on game day if they're scrambling around to find a stand-in. Even if there's no assignment, they may remember you next time there's a problem.

TEAMWORK AND TRUST

In NHL hockey, there are four on-ice officials: two referees and two linesmen. NBA basketball games have three referees, one near the baseline, one near the sideline, and one near midcourt. The four umpires on a Major League Baseball crew cover home plate and the three bases. They also rotate positions each game.

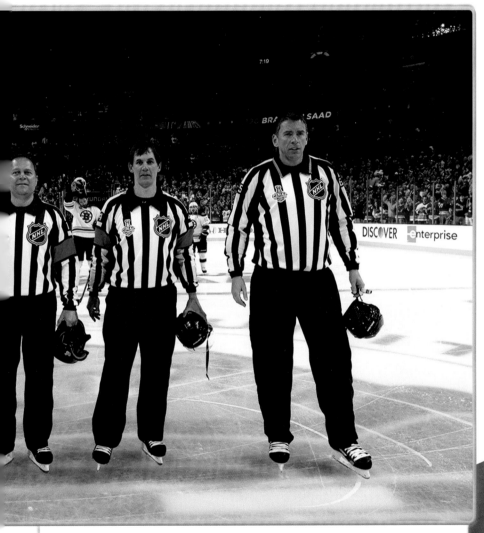

The third team on the ice—a hockey officiating crew—stops for a picture before a Stanley Cup game.

In the NFL and other football leagues, there are seven officials. The referee is in charge of an umpire, head linesman, line judge, side judge, field judge, and back judge. Unlike baseball umpires, they don't rotate at their positions. Major League Soccer has four officials, including a referee who is in charge of the crew.

The people that an official needs to get to know best are the members of his or her own team. Crew members don't have to be best of friends, but they should try to be the best of teammates, and it's essential that they get to know and understand each other.

Pregame meetings and postgame evaluations help officials work out disagreements and misunderstandings and learn what to expect of each other. Professional officials take these meetings seriously—although sometimes with a little humor.

Ed Hochuli, one of the best-known NFL officials, meets with his seven-man field crew, plus the replay official and video operator, for several hours before each game. In addition to being graded on every play by NFL staff, the team members are evaluated by Hochuli on their previous performances.

Hochuli has been known to hand out toys—rubber ducks, bears, or one- and two-dollar bills—as prizes or

Referee Ed Hochuli is not only one of the top officials in the NFL. He's known for being an excellent teacher to the members of his officiating crew.

booby prizes to crew members who made good calls, or not so good ones, during the previous game. He also hands out encouragement, criticism, and advice. A *USA Today* reporter told how Hochuli once awarded himself

STAYING IN SHAPE

One of the highlights at the NBA All-Star Game weekend in 2007 was when Hall of Fame forward Charles Barkley barely beat referee Dick Bavetta in a race of three and a half court sprints. Working as an analyst for the television network TNT, Barkley had made a crack on the air about the physical condition of one of the oldest and smallest refs ever in the league. Bavetta and Barkley agreed to race as a stunt to benefit charity.

Barkley had a good lead in the race, but he started clowning at the finish. Bavetta dived head first across center court and came close to winning. Barkley was forty-three years old at that time, and Bavetta was sixty-seven.

"I honestly thought I could win," Bavetta said at a press conference after the race. Bavetta became the longest-serving referee in the NBA thanks in part to a rigorous training routine. He's an example of what getting in shape and staying there can do for an official's career.

Bavetta started as a basketball referee in amateur and high school leagues in New York and worked his way up to a minor pro league. For nine years, he tried out for the NBA and was rejected every time because he looked frail and unimposing.

He finally made it into the league in 1975. During his first seasons he got low performance evaluations. To improve, he worked off-season games in New Jersey and at Rucker Park, the legendary center of playground basketball in Harlem. He also started a rigorous training schedule. And he kept studying the rule book.

Within a few years, Bavetta was recognized as one of the best referees in the NBA. In 1980 he was

Referee Dick Bavetta lost his 2007 footrace with Charles Barkley, but he was the last man standing. Thanks to excellent physical conditioning, Bavetta has officiated more NBA games than anyone.

named as a chief referee. By 2000, he was one of the highest paid officials in the NBA, earning more than $200,000 a year. In 2013, Bavetta officiated his 2,600th consecutive game, more than any official in the league's history.

the booby prize, a plumber's plunger, because he felt that he'd called the worst game of anyone.

"He's pretty thorough, but if you notice, he's doing a lot of teaching in there," Johnny Grier, an NFL supervisor of officials, told the newspaper.

Teamwork can be important off the field, too. Professional officials are reluctant to criticize their colleagues in public. In some situations, they must also look out for each other's physical safety. Hardly a season passes without news reports of a sports official being assaulted by fans or a player, sometimes even killed.

Officials need to trust their teammates, but they must also keep the trust of the coaches, players, and fans. They must have what the National Association of Sports Officials (NASO) calls "strong moral character and integrity." The NASO says in its "A Covenant with Sports Officials" that "officials must be fair minded and courageous," and they should adhere to the officials' code of conduct.

If people can't trust sports officials, it stands to reason they won't trust the sport. Officials' calls may be booed and second-guessed, and errors may be magnified, but basically people believe that games are being called honestly, or they wouldn't believe in the integrity of the sport. Many people would lose interest. "Sports officials bear great responsibility for engendering public confidence in sports," the covenant says.

There have been scandals of all sorts sprinkled through the history of most sports, but relatively few have involved cheating by officials. In 2007 an NBA official was sentenced to jail for selling inside information to gamblers before games. It was reported in 2013 that a Major League umpire was fired after failing a drug test.

CONTINUING EDUCATION

Is a college education important for an officiating career? Many colleges and universities give courses in officiating sports, but they don't have majors or degrees in officiating. A college degree isn't required to become an official, although it certainly doesn't hurt. Sports leagues and conferences mostly require just a high school diploma in the way of formal education.

Becoming a good official is more a matter of continuing education—taking every opportunity to work a game or scrimmage, talking to more experienced officials, and constantly studying the rules.

There are officiating schools and training camps for officials in all the major sports, and sooner or later an official who wants to move up the ladder will probably want to attend one of them.

Colleges, particularly community colleges, sometimes offer short courses in officiating various sports. Some of these programs also give certifications to officiate in their states. In addition, leagues and associations conduct clinics, seminars, rules updates, and training in the off-season. Some of these are required attendance for anyone who wants to be an official in the program.

However, a college degree—in any field, not just in sports—can be important to an officiating career in other ways. The vast majority of sports officials have other jobs simply because officiating doesn't pay enough year-round to make a living. Many of those jobs require degrees.

Even well-paid officials in the NFL are professionals in other fields, holding such positions as lawyer, computer systems analyst, high school teacher, and probation officer, among others. For an official who wants to move up in his or her sport, being a successful, responsible professional looks good on the résumé.

College courses can also help officials' performance on the field. Umpires and referees need to be good communicators and listeners. Subjects such as speech and psychology, especially sports psychology, can teach officials important skills they can use in game situations.

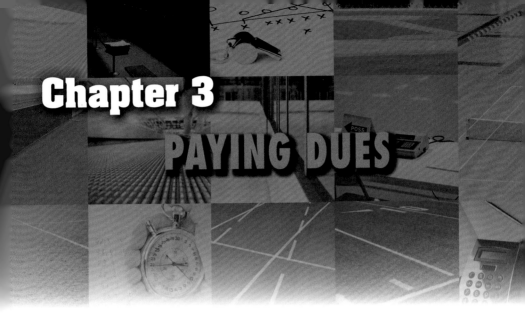

Chapter 3
PAYING DUES

Starting at the bottom will usually mean doing volunteer work at games for young players in sports such as T-ball or flag football. Then an official may want to move up to more organized Little League or youth league games. There won't be much pay along the way, if there's any at all.

The national Little League organization, for example, says it doesn't see why its umpires should be paid. To qualify for the Little League World Series, umpires must not only be the best in their regions, they must be able to show that they haven't taken any money during the season.

So newcomers have to study the rules, learn the mechanics, handle stressful situations, and donate their time so that the players can play—and do it all without getting paid. It's enough to make a new official ask, "How much do I really love this game?"

Most officials love it a lot. And if you care about a sport, what better place is there to be than close to the

Most officials, especially in youth leagues, are volunteers who get little or no pay. Little League World Series umpires must be able to show that they haven't taken any money during the season.

action? Volunteer sports officials also get the personal satisfaction of knowing that they're helping the players, the fans, and their communities, even though most of them don't make a big deal out of it.

Many referees and umpires who do get good salaries are generous off the field, giving their time and money to community causes. As a group, sports officials aren't selfish when it comes to helping others. It's what the job is all about, after all.

UMPIRING LEGENDS

Of the three hundred players, coaches, executives, and pioneers in the Baseball Hall of Fame, only ten are umpires. They weren't inducted because of batting averages or pitching prowess, but because of the style, integrity, and dedication they brought to the game.

- Al Barlick reached the major leagues at the age of twenty-five in 1940 and retired in 1971. His career included twenty-seven seasons in the National League.

- Nestor Chylak was a decorated World War II veteran who joined the American League in 1954 and umpired for twenty-six seasons.

- Jocko Conlan became an umpire by accident. During a 1935 White Sox–Browns game he was asked to substitute for an umpire who was overcome by heat, and he began his full-time career the following year. He was in the National League from 1941 to 1964.

- Tom Connoly started in the National League in the early days of baseball and later worked the very first American League game on April 24, 1901. He became the league's first umpire-in-chief after retiring from fieldwork.

- Billy Evans was the youngest umpire in major league history at age twenty-two. He umpired from 1906 through 1927 and then was an executive for various clubs.

SIDEBAR CONTINUES ON NEXT PAGE

- Doug Harvey was a crew chief for eighteen of his thirty-one seasons in the National League. Harvey stressed the importance of timing and was known for his firm control of games. Harvey was mentor to a new generation of young umpires.

- Cal Hubbard spent eight seasons in the minors and worked in the American League from 1936 until 1951. He was the first person ever inducted into three major sports shrines, including the College and Pro Football Halls of Fame.

Hall of Famer Bill McGowan was known as an "iron man" among umpires. He worked 2,541 games over sixteen years without missing an inning.

- Bill Klem's nickname was "the Old Arbitrator." He always worked behind the plate because of his superior ability to call pitches. He worked for thirty-seven years in the National League. After retiring from the field he became the league's first modern chief of umpires.

- Bill McGowan was known for his colorful style during a thirty-year career in the American League. McGowan was an iron man among umps.

He worked a stretch of sixteen years—2,541 games—without missing an inning.

- Hank O'Day was a former Major League player who umpired ten World Series in the early 1900s and was also a manager in the major leagues.

DEVELOPING SKILLS AND MENTAL TOUGHNESS

Sports psychologists say that athletes who succeed at the top levels of their sport have a certain trait in common. They call it mental toughness. Successful officials have it, too. It's not something people are born with. It must be learned and practiced just like other sports skills.

Mental toughness is the ability to focus and make quick decisions despite pressure and distractions. It's what puts players "in the zone." They don't have to think about how to do the next right thing, they just do it. It's the ability to shut out fear, doubt, and indecision. There are all kinds of theories about where mental toughness comes from and what it really is. However, experts say there are several things that athletes and officials can do to develop it.

The referee takes a decisive stance during a lacrosse game in Hamilton, Canada. Developing mental toughness is as important for officials as it is for players.

The most important ingredient is motivation. Sure, every athlete wants to win, and every official wants to do a perfect job of calling the game. But how badly do they want it? Badly enough to endure long days of conditioning? To keep running even after it starts to hurt? To keep studying rules even though you've read them all before and you're tired and bored?

Another ingredient is preparation. When someone repeats a routine over and over, it eventually becomes automatic, and nothing imparts confidence like practice. When it's time to perform that action for real, there's no need to think about it. The body seems to take over, leaving the mind free to think about the next move.

Visualization is a widely used preparation tool. It means using all your senses to imagine yourself doing your job perfectly, or possibly imagining how it will feel after you've done it well. Athletes in all sports use it, and it works for everyday situations, too. Using all the senses to imagine doing a skill strengthens the neural pathways that are used when you do the skill in real life.

Visualization, or mental rehearsal, can be used before, during, and after actual games. An official might imagine herself at the end of a hard match. She's tired and in danger of losing her focus. She visualizes getting a second wind, pushing through the fatigue, and being in perfect position to make a crucial call at the end of the game.

Visualization becomes easier with practice, and it's described in many books and articles on mental toughness. For beginners, experts recommend relaxing in a quiet spot, closing your eyes, and imagining a scene with all the senses. How does the grass smell? Is the weather hot? Is there a lot of crowd noise? When visualizing a technique or skill it may help to play the mental images in slow motion, making sure every step is executed perfectly.

One way to visualize is externally, that is to see yourself from the outside as if you were watching on film. Another is internally, as if you were really seeing and feeling the things around you from your own perspective.

Routine and ritual—performing the same actions in the same way again and again—can help focus the mind and body.

Visualization can also be done in game situations. For example, a football official may anticipate a pass on the next play and, if there's time, he may visualize how he will turn, where he will be looking, and the steps he will take to get into position for a call.

Ritual is another technique that many credit with boosting their mental toughness. Many athletes and officials go through the same routines before games: arriving at the stadium at a certain time, using a certain door, dressing in a certain way, right sock before left. Ritual is a routine that can trigger muscle memory, signaling the body that it's time to perform.

Ritual is often used during games, by officials and athletes alike. A basketball player may dribble three times—always three times—before shooting a free throw. A home plate umpire between batters might reset his ball-strike indicator, check the position of the base umpires, then check his indicator again and adjust his chest protector before crouching to call the next pitch. It's nothing that the fans would notice. However, when the same actions are done in the same order, time after time, ritual can help focus the body as well as the mind.

These mental toughness techniques are often used in workouts as well as in game situations. They can help athletes and officials through the tough physical conditioning they need to succeed. Conditioning itself is a major mental toughness ingredient. No athlete or official succeeds without being in shape. Getting in shape—putting in the work—helps create the confidence that's a big part of mental toughness.

Developing mental toughness isn't just for those who want to succeed in sports. It's something that can help a person achieve excellence in whatever he or she does. That's also true of the other qualities that go into making a good sports official. What are some of those other qualities? They include good decision making, communication skills, confidence, poise under pressure, the ability to deal with conflict, and sound mechanics.

Being decisive seems to come more naturally to some people than to others, but it's a quality that can be developed with practice. Psychologists say fear is a problem for many people who have trouble making quick decisions—they hesitate because they're afraid of making the wrong one.

Preparation, including a thorough knowledge of the rules, can help an official have the confidence he or she needs to be more decisive. So can practice. When you rehearse an action, either in real life or by visualization, it's easier to do the action under pressure. One of the things that officials work hardest on is getting into position to see the play and make the call. It's a lot easier to be decisive when you've seen what happened and you know it.

Communication works two ways. Good officials have to be good listeners, first of all in training. Studying the rules is essential, but learning the game also means listening

Officials have to be good communicators. That means knowing the mechanics of proper signals as well as the right way to talk to players and coaches.

with an open mind to mentors, instructors, and other officials. During a game, a coach may "give a referee an earful" because he's angry about a call, but he may also have a valid point. Veteran officials know how to listen without interruption and when it's time to end the discussion.

They also communicate their decisions clearly, through the sport's regulation hand and arm signals and verbally when it's appropriate. Some gestures and body language aren't in the officials' manuals, but they're customary in the sport and they make sense. If a coach yells, "He's holding my guy!" a referee might raise a hand briefly to give a little signal that he's heard and will be watching.

When it comes to talking, players, coaches, and others must always be addressed with respect, even if they're being disrespectful. Explanations should be short, to the point, and as simple as possible.

KEEPING COOL IN CONFLICT

It's natural to get rattled when there's a lot at stake and things are moving fast—especially if thousands of people are watching, players are fired up, and a coach is disputing your judgment. Good officials can keep their cool under that kind of pressure. Experience helps, of course. If you've been in the situation many times before, it's probably not as tough to stay poised as it was the first few times.

TOMMY NUÑEZ

"I was a nobody all of my life," Tommy Nuñez says on his foundation's Web site, "it's nice to be a somebody."

Nuñez got to be "somebody" by becoming one of the best referees in basketball. He started out officiating amateur games in Arizona and ended up in the NBA. Nuñez was the first Mexican American referee in any major U.S. pro sport.

He got off to a shaky start. As a teenager in Phoenix, Arizona, Nuñez was expelled from high school, got kicked out of the Phoenix Boys Club, and ran into trouble with the law. Eventually he was given a choice: do military service, or do jail time. He chose the Marines.

Nuñez got his high school diploma while he was serving in Okinawa in the Marine Corps. He left the service determined to do better at something, although he wasn't quite sure what. Back home in Phoenix, he began refereeing basketball games for $3.50 an hour.

"Nobody would come to those games," he said later. "But it was in my neighborhood and I needed the money."

As he got more experience officiating, Nuñez started working high school and junior college games. His break came when an NBA official saw him work a Phoenix Suns exhibition game and suggested he try out for the league.

At first he said no. He had a day job as a telephone repairman and didn't want to leave his "comfort zone" in Phoenix. Then he changed his mind and agreed to go to the league tryout in 1972. Out of one thousand applicants, sixteen were picked, and Nuñez was one of them. He went on to officiate in the NBA for thirty years and then worked for the league as a supervisor of officials.

After retiring, he traveled the country encouraging kids to stay in school, stay out of trouble, and participate in sports. The National Hispanic Basketball Classic tournament started in 1980, and since then the Tommy Nuñez Scholarship and Youth Activities Foundation has funded events and sponsored tournaments for young people. It also awards scholarships.

"If I can make it, you can make it!" he tells kids. "Stay in school!" The Phoenix gym where Nuñez got his start is now named for him.

Here's where all the preparation, practice, visualization, and mental toughness can really pay off. Sometimes the best performances of a game go unnoticed. They are when an official coolly sorts out a hot problem and signals for play to go on.

Team sports are organized forms of conflict, and people who play them get emotional. It's an official's job to manage the conflict, and it's easier in some sports than others. Fighting is common at most levels of Canadian and U.S. hockey. That disgusts some people, and it delights others, but fistfights and team enforcers are a tradition as old as the sport.

So it's not surprising that hockey officials have written procedures on how to manage fights. The guidelines tell linesmen how to approach a brawl, and how to handle fighting players, separate them, and get them to the penalty box. The referee has the assignment of keeping other players clear, writing down numbers, and handing out penalties.

Hockey is the only major team sport where fighting doesn't mean an automatic ejection from the game. Experienced officials in other sports may not have these procedures spelled out for them, but they do know ways to manage conflict and keep it from getting out of hand. This is sometimes called "preventive" officiating.

Officials sometimes have to break up fights, especially in hockey. However, good officials work on preventing them.

It means knowing the signs that a problem is brewing. Are the players getting frustrated? Is the coach yelling at his team and assistants? It means thinking before speaking, and it means having a set of "tools" for heading off trouble before it happens. In the book *Successful Sports Officiating*, editors of *Referee* magazine and the National Association of Sports Officials have several suggestions.

One of them is to have the "presence" of an official. Look athletic and confident, wear a proper uniform that fits, and look like you belong. Keep emotion out of your voice. Don't make threats. Find common ground with coaches by pointing out a shared goal, such as "Let's keep the game safe." Don't argue. Be truthful, even if you have to let a player or coach know that you're aware you missed a call. Never say things like "It's just a game" to players or coaches because they might think you don't care.

No official likes to have a reputation as someone who can't control his or her games. That makes it harder to find games in the future. In many leagues it also results in extra paperwork. Officials may have to write game reports or misconduct reports when there are serious incidents or when they have to eject players and coaches. They'd much rather prevent the trouble in the first place.

There are lots of books, manuals, and articles on mental toughness, preventing conflict, and tips and tricks of officiating. For beginners, some of the best tips come from other officials at the games and scrimmages they're working, or from a mentor.

Schools, clinics, and workshops are required for officials to work in lots of leagues. They're designed to be demanding but fun. Trainees not only work on rules and mechanics, they get to know each other, work together as a team, hang out, and learn about the profession. Some clinics may last only a weekend.

A course at one of the professional schools may last two months or longer. Students get written as well as on-field instruction, and they spend a lot of time calling scrimmages and actual games.

Training is just as important for officials as it is for players. This team is shown working out for the 2010 World Cup Soccer final in South Africa.

For those who make it into the college ranks, the NCAA hosts off-season clinics for officials, with special rates at good hotels in locations all over the country. These are usually organized by regions, such as northeast, southeast, west, and central United States so that officials from one conference get to work out and swap information with officials from other areas.

Clinics and camps for referees and umpires are also great places to meet and be seen by talent scouts—the officials from conferences, officials' associations, schools, and any others who may have a say in handing out game assignments.

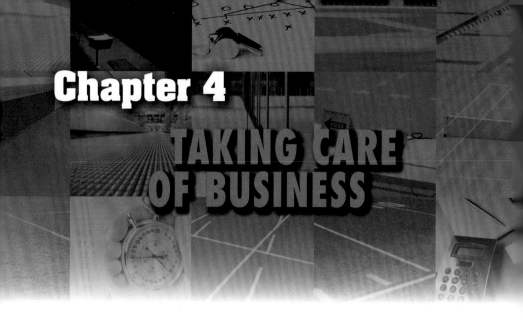

Chapter 4

TAKING CARE OF BUSINESS

In the long run, being a success or failure in the officiating game depends on how well you make decisions, communicate with players and coaches, and manage games. But there's also business involved, especially for officials who want to work with school sports. To work school games, officials must be registered with the state office that regulates interscholastic sports.

Referees and umpires in most leagues—especially amateur leagues—are "independent contractors." That means that legally they are self-employed. They volunteer or hire out their services for pay, often on a game-by-game basis. Even though they may belong to an officials' association, or do most of their work in one league, they're probably not employees of the association or league.

Other examples of contract employees are a mechanic who fixes cars or an independent accountant who does people's taxes; they get paid by the job. This way of working has its advantages and disadvantages.

One big advantage is that independent contractors can decide how much work they want to take on. They don't have to show up at an office every day and take orders from a boss. That's important because most officials have day jobs that produce most of their income. Some professional officials at the upper levels of sport can make enough from refereeing or umpiring to support their families. They're a minority, though.

There are also certain responsibilities and disadvantages, too. Independent contractors have to arrange for their own health care. They have to keep track of their income and pay taxes on it. They usually should have some sort of liability insurance to cover them in case they're blamed for neglecting something or making a mistake that results in harm or damage to someone else. They also need to find game assignments. Officials' associations can help with most of these issues.

HOW DO I GET ASSIGNED TO GAMES?

Just about every city and region of the country has a local officials' association, and some places have several of them. Many local officials' organizations work with schools, leagues, and recreational programs to provide umpires and referees for their games. Many have training and mentoring programs for beginning officials, and they may also arrange clinics and workshops to keep officials up to date on rules and techniques.

Getting game assignments means making a good impression on game and tournament organizers. These referees are trying out for the Women's World Cup.

Some local organizations have responsibility for assigning officials to games. In other places, game assignments may be the decision of a school or league administrator. This person may have the job title of coordinator, supervisor, or assignor. However the assignments are made, local organizations are usually the best place for a new official to find out how the system works and the best way to go about getting game assignments.

It's always a good idea to have a résumé ready to show someone. Assignors need to know who you are, where to find you, and what you've done. A résumé is usually a single sheet of paper listing your contact information, age, experience, education, and any training you've had in officiating.

Having friends and acquaintances in the right places can also be important, but in some places officials are not allowed to contact conference or league officials directly to ask for refereeing jobs. The reason for this practice is to ensure fairness and avoid conflicts of interest.

Many local officials' organizations are more than just places to find jobs. There are other advantages to joining. Local organizations may act as support groups for members who are dealing with questions about pay or safety. Some organizations have guidelines for talking with coaches and players during games, or lists of things that should be done to prepare for a game. They may insist on decent dressing rooms for referees or have guidelines in place to make sure officials get paid on time.

Most sports also have national officials' associations. The National Association of Sports Officials (NASO) is the main officials' organization in the United States. It has nineteen thousand members who work in practically all sports, at all levels.

The NASO Web site has a lot of information about the group's programs. It includes articles on how to become an official and information on insurance coverage, training sessions for officials in the various sports, state laws regarding independent contractors, and laws protecting officials from assault. NASO is also affiliated with the monthly magazine *Referee*, which has news and feature articles about officiating around the country. The publishers of *Referee* also produce books and articles about legal and business issues of concern to officials.

STATE ASSOCIATIONS

State interscholastic associations regulate how sports are played between schools. Every state has one. Many of these associations also oversee activities such as band and debate. They decide on things like rules for player eligibility and how many games may be played in a sport each season. Officials must register with their state association in order to work at school games.

There's a list of state associations on the Web site of the National Federation of State High School Associations. (NFHS) These associations make the regulations for officials. They decide on the requirements for becoming an official, what it takes to officiate at playoffs and championships, and what officials must do to be registered in their state.

Usually that means paying a fee and passing a test. There's usually an age limit as well. In Florida, for example, officials must be eighteen or older, although that state has a Student Officials Program for sixteen- and seventeen-year-olds.

Many state associations leave it to local officials' organizations to train and certify new officials. It may sound complicated, but it's usually just a matter of contacting your state organization to find out what the requirements are in your area. It may be as simple as going to a game and asking an official to point you in the right direction. He or she will likely put you in touch with the local officials' association, and that's usually the best place to start.

NATIONAL ASSOCIATIONS

The National Federation of State High School Associations represents the governing bodies for high school sports in all fifty U.S. states. It mostly serves the schools, but it also decides on rules that affect officials and provides other products and services, such as rulebooks and manuals for officials.

The federation decides on officials' uniforms and makes them available for sale. It also provides insurance for officials, although most states also have their own insurance policies for registered officials. These policies usually cover injuries that happen during games and liability issues. There's an "NFHS Officiating Central Hub" on the NFHS Web site, although you need to register to access most of the information.

Most referee and umpire jobs in the near future will be in high school and especially women's sports, and most states make it easy for you to get your own game organized, without much paperwork. In some states, depending on the sport, you can find out the qualifications, get officials' handbooks, take the test, and pay the fee online. For example, check out the Frequently Asked Questions page on the Illinois High School Association's Web site. The procedures are simple and straightforward. You can even be licensed online as an Illinois official—although you're on probation until you pass the test and work out on the field at a clinic. More and more associations are making it easier to find local games online and stay in touch.

STAYING ORGANIZED

Gene Steratore is noted for working his way into the top ranks of officiating in two sports at the same time. He started refereeing YMCA basketball games near Pittsburgh at age eleven and became a referee in NCAA Division I basketball and a referee in the NFL. In an interview with the *New York Times*, he recalled how he was paid "a quarter and a chocolate pop" for working his first games.

It's nice to be paid, even if it isn't much. However doing a part-time or year-round job of officiating means you're in business; and since officials are independent contractors, you're in charge of your own business.

You're the boss! But you're also the secretary, who has to make sure the employee (you) and your gear get to the

Gene Steratore worked his way to the top ranks of officiating in two sports: NCAA basketball and NFL football.

park on time, so the employee can focus on the game and do a good job for the company (you). Also somebody has to take care of personal medical insurance and liability insurance, sign work contracts, keep track of income and expenses, pay any taxes, and schedule time for it all.

Since you're the boss, you don't have to do it all your-self. Associations can help with details such as insurance, and there may be others who can help—professionals such as accountants or a friend or relative who cares about your career. One way or another, however, it's the boss's responsibility to see that it all gets handled.

The game gets more complicated for officials who have school schedules or job schedules to juggle. Time management is an important skill for officials both in games and in real life. Games may be just a couple of hours long, but an officials' job takes more time than most people realize.

There has to be time for travel, time for pregame meetings, time to suit up and warm up, and time to check the grounds or the court. There also has to be time to learn how to do these things. No official wants a reputation as someone who's late for games or worse—who doesn't show up.

For two-sport official Gene Steratore, football games start in August, and basketball games end in March, and there's a hectic travel schedule when they overlap in the winter. It's not much easier for officials who have full-time jobs.

Income is subject to state and federal taxes. However equipment costs,

Steratore in action at an NCAA basketball game. For two-sport officials, life can get hectic when seasons overlap. Good time management is essential.

fees, hotel costs, travel costs, and other job expenses are all deductible. It helps to have an accountant, but you're responsible for keeping track of it all. Officials usually work under employment contracts that they must read, understand, and sign. These official agreements may be between the official and the school or conference that's hosting the games. Or they may be between the official and his or her local association.

Contracts work both ways. They spell out your responsibilities and the responsibility of the association or schools where you officiate. Some contracts are fairly simple to read through and some may be long and complicated, but it's important to understand them. Fortunately they are standard for most officials, so it's not hard to ask for help from a colleague or someone in your association.

If you get injured during a game, who pays the medical bills? What if you accidentally injure a player? Medical insurance for officials is provided through the NFHS Officials Association and is also provided by some state associations. However it's always a good idea to have your own medical insurance. Liability insurance—the kind you need if you're blamed for hurting someone else or being at fault for damage—is also provided by some state associations and schools and the NFHS Officials Association.

A PIONEER OF AMERICAN SOCCER

Robert Evans grew up playing soccer in Wales, in the United Kingdom, and went on to become one of the most respected soccer referees in America. He's an example of how athletes can become outstanding students as well as outstanding officials.

Evans graduated from college with a degree in geology and moved to Canada to continue his studies, earning a master's degree. Living in Nova Scotia, he broke a leg while playing in a local league game, and while he was on the mend, he studied the Laws of the Game, the rules governing soccer.

Evans qualified as a referee but also stayed in school and kept playing. He moved to Kansas, where he earned a Ph.D. degree in geology and was player-coach of the University of Kansas soccer team.

Evans's work as a research geologist took him to Texas in 1969. Soccer still wasn't a very big sport in the United States at that time, and Evans thought his soccer career was over. However, he was soon invited to be player-coach of a local team. He was also one of a handful of qualified soccer refs in Texas, and he began teaching refereeing to others.

The first version of the North American Soccer League began in 1968, and the new league needed trained officials. Evans worked in the league from 1972 until it folded in 1985.

He also traveled overseas, refereeing international matches for the World Cup and Olympics. In 1988 he was named national director of referee instruction for the U.S. Soccer Federation.

Evans finally settled with this family in California, where he wrote articles about his scientific specialty, as well as about soccer. He wrote *Manual for Linesmen* and coauthored *Teaching Offside*, how-to books for referees, as well as articles about the game. In 1992 he became the first American appointed as a referee instructor by FIFA, the International Federation of Association Football. He has won several national awards for his contributions to American soccer.

HANDLING CRITICISM

Being criticized by fans is just part of an official's job, and most good officials shrug it off. Taking criticism and coaching from professional evaluators is part of the job, too, and good officials use it to get better.

After every NFL game, officials start watching videos of their work, from every available camera angle. The referee studies how the judges and linesmen on his crew handled every play and gives them grades. League evaluators are also watching each official on each play and grading the performance.

In the league's grading system, officials get points for good calls and lose points for bad calls. The ones with the best grades at the end of the season make it to the playoffs.

Officials review plays during games, but after the game their own performance will be reviewed. Good officials say criticism and evaluation help them get better.

When you count the fans in the stands and the millions who watch on TV, it's easily one of the most scrutinized jobs in the world.

Officials are second-guessed so much by fans and coaches that it might be tempting sometimes to just turn off all criticism. However criticism, when it comes from impartial experts, isn't a bad thing.

Performance evaluations are standard for employees in most jobs, and many employees don't like being told their weak points. However, high-level sports officials say they welcome evaluations and expert criticism because it helps them improve their game.

Criticism and evaluation take place for officials at every level of sport. Conferences and school associations use former officials to evaluate their current ones. For small college and high school officials, the grading systems may not be as elaborate as the NFL's. However, even state high school associations can be very specific about what's expected of their officials in each sport.

For example, the Iowa Girls High School Athletic Union has a list of standards for its officials that is nearly three pages long. It covers pregame and postgame responsibilities as well as professional manner and poise; communication with coaches, players, scorer's table personnel, and other referees; game awareness, game control, and the "flow" of games; accuracy and consistency in calling violations and fouls; coverage on and off the ball; rules knowledge and penalty administration; signals, positioning, and floor coverage; and appearance, fitness, and conditioning. It's a long list.

Performance evaluations for officials are usually kept confidential, just as they are for employees in other jobs. Their work is very public however, and sports leagues like to assure the public that they're fielding the best officials possible. The Union of European Football Associations (UEFA) posted a series of Web videos about the inside world of soccer officials. One of them, titled "Dealing With Decisions," offers an inside look at how top-level officials are evaluated and how to handle criticism professionally.

It's about a three-man officials' team covering a big international match between Poland and Austria. It shows game action, an exciting goal, and the crowd on its feet roaring.

After the game the officials meet privately with a UEFA referee's observer. He tells them that replays showed an offside on that crucial goal. It shouldn't have been allowed. The offside was pretty obvious to everyone, he tells them. It was on the big screen at the stadium.

The league official compliments the team on their control of the game and tells them they did a good job. But, he says: "I cannot ignore the pictures.... It's a pity these things happen." The UEFA official continues, "It's our life, boys. It's our life." There's a more formal debriefing later, and an expert goes over film with the team. He points out the violation and stops the action, and everyone studies the positioning of the linesman responsible for the call.

The linesman says he was out of position, and now he sees it clearly for the first time. "I'm completely rooted to the corner flag," he says. "I have no idea why."

When the team shows up later at a meeting of other officials and UEFA organizers, it's announced that they're leaving. They get a round of applause and handshakes and tokens of thanks for their work, but they're out of the tournament. The video is part of a film titled "Les Arbitres" ("The Referees") on the UEFA Web site.

Chapter 5
WHAT IT TAKES

Starting out as a youth sports official can be easy, but there are requirements that vary from league to league, town to town, and state to state. Moving up to junior varsity and high school level naturally takes more study and practice.

Only experienced officials make it into the college ranks, and moving from small college play to the big NCAA games can take an entire career. A few elite officials make it to the big professional leagues, if they're very good, very determined, and very dedicated. It also helps to be lucky.

Overall, the number of sports officiating jobs in the United States will keep increasing at least until 2020, according to the BLS. The bureau expects that paid jobs for umpires, referees, and other officials will grow 20 percent between 2010 and 2020. That's faster than the average of all other jobs in the country.

The number of jobs available for referees and umpires is expected to keep increasing over the next few years, but competition for the top jobs will always be tough.

The main reason is that population is increasing, and that means there will be more schools and more sports activities—and thus a need for more sports officials. Some schools with troubled budgets may consider reducing their sports programs, but sports are so popular that parents, fund-raisers, and booster clubs will likely help if school money is short, the bureau says.

For high school officials, the job outlook is really good. The best opportunities are for officials who want to work in high school sports and women's sports in high school and college, the bureau says. Competition for jobs will always be tough for the top college assignments and even tougher for professional jobs.

BASEBALL AND SOFTBALL UMPIRES

Here are some details about umpiring in youth leagues and Little League, high school, college, and the minor and major leagues.

YOUTH LEAGUES AND LITTLE LEAGUE

Youth leagues are always on the lookout for qualified volunteers to fill their umpire positions, and many of them have training programs for people who want to be officials. A background check may be necessary, and you may have to take a rules test.

The age requirement for umpires in many leagues is sixteen, although some leagues have umpires as young as thirteen—just past the limit for playing Little League baseball. In Little League, the local president is usually the one responsible for appointing umpires, for approval by the league's directors.

Some leagues may furnish equipment and training materials for umpires to use. In other places, umpires must furnish their own. For a small fee you can sign up with Little League Baseball's Umpire Registry. Members receive rulebooks for baseball and softball, a uniform patch, a certificate of membership, training materials, and other benefits.

HIGH SCHOOL

High school umpires usually have to buy their own uniforms and equipment. You can buy a basic starter set—shirt, pants, chest protector, mask, shin guards, shoes, and other tools for under $300 new, less for used gear.

Other starting-out costs include fees for joining your local officials' association and for licensing or certification. These fees aren't very high, usually about $25 to $50.

State interscholastic associations usually require prospective umpires to attend a training camp, have a background check, and pass a rules test before they can be certified. Some programs pay officials' travel expenses and some don't. A high school umpire who wants to can work hundreds of games in a season.

COLLEGE

College conferences require their umpires to pass a test and to have several years of experience, usually in high school ball, before they can be certified. Some smaller conferences will accept minor league experience or graduation from a professional umpire school. College officials must be members of an accredited umpires' organization.

Students study rules at the Jim Evans Academy of Professional Umpiring. Umpires in the major and minor leagues must graduate from a school that's recognized by Major League Baseball.

There's also an NCAA rules exam and an on-field mechanics test that most applicants must pass.

College umpires naturally have to travel farther than high school umpires, and the road schedule can be tough during the season. College umpires are expected to attend off-season clinics to keep up with rule changes and stay on top of their game.

MINOR LEAGUES

Minor league umpires must graduate from an umpire school that's recognized by Major League Baseball. Top

Professional umpire training includes classroom work, training sessions like this one with instructors, and calling games and scrimmages.

graduates are invited to take an evaluation course for a job in the minor leagues. Those who make the grade in umpire school can start in the Rookie League and try to work their way up from there. It's a long way up.

The next step is to the Class A leagues, and from there to the Double-A and Triple-A leagues. Upcoming players can skip leagues on their way to the majors, but umpires have to work their way up through each one.

Life can be grueling during the season, especially because of the travel demands: driving or flying to the next game, finding a decent hotel you can afford, and getting to the next game several hundred miles away. On its Web site, the Association of Minor League Umpires calls its members "the hardest working employees of the national past time." Those who stick with it all the way up to Triple-A ball are on the doorstep of the majors.

MAJOR LEAGUES

Major league umpires spend eight to twelve years in the minors and must reach Triple-A level before they're even considered for one of the seventy major league umpire jobs. Years may pass before there's an opening. On the other hand, the pay is great.

FOOTBALL

Whether you're starting at the bottom or moving up the ladder, don't be insulted if you're asked to work the chains or if you're asked to be a line judge or back judge instead of being the referee. Officials in football have to earn their positions every step of the way, just as players and coaches do.

YOUTH, RECREATION, AND LITTLE LEAGUES

The first step is to sign up with your local recreation league and ask about their requirements. These are slightly different everywhere, but they're probably not very rigorous. Many community and youth leagues have weekend clinics and workouts where new officials can learn the basics, so they're great places to start.

There will probably be a background check, and you may have to pass a test on rules—especially local league rules. Just about every community has its own variations on the official rulebook. In many leagues you must be sixteen or older to officiate.

HIGH SCHOOL

State interscholastic associations usually require officials to be a member of their local officials' organization, have a background check, pass a rules test, and be certified before they may call high school games. Certification through USA Football, an organization dedicated to the development of youth football in partnership with the NFL, may also be recognized. The membership fee is about $25.

COLLEGE

When it comes to college football, most people think of the NCAA. However, there's no single place to sign up to become a college football official. Referees, linesmen, and judges for college and university football games are hired by athletic conferences, and there are dozens of conferences.

Each one has its own application process and requirements. Most of them require several years of high school experience. Applicants must belong to an accredited officials' association.

The NCAA is grouped into three divisions according to the size of member schools, and officials without college experience aren't likely to be hired by the bigger conferences in Division I. Beginners usually apply to Division II or Division III conferences.

However, conferences in the National Association of Intercollegiate Athletics (NAIA) can also be starting points. It's probably even easier to find games in a conference of junior or community colleges, and the games will likely be closer to home.

NFL

Applicants must have a minimum ten years experience as an official, and five of those years must be at the varsity college level or with another professional league, such as the Canadian Football League. They must be a member of an accredited officials' association or be a former player or coach.

A STANDING OVATION FOR OFFICIALS

There's no substitute for the years of experience, training, and study that it takes to become a top-level official. Most of the time fans, coaches, and players don't appreciate that, but sometimes it becomes obvious.

One of those times came at the beginning of the 2012 NFL season. Team owners and the league "locked out" the regular officials because they didn't agree on the terms of a new work contract. The lockout meant that experienced league officials could not work games. Instead the league hired replacement officials, mostly from small college and even high school leagues. The result was a near disaster. The replacements worked the first three weeks of the season, and each week there were more complaints about missed calls and sloppy games.

The last straw came on *Monday Night Football* when the Seattle Seahawks defeated the Green Bay Packers 14–12 because a replacement official missed a call on the final play of the game. Outraged fans and media demanded that something be done.

Two days later, the league and the officials agreed on a work contract covering the next several years. When regular officials took the field in Baltimore for their first game between the Ravens and the Cleveland Browns, they got a standing ovation. Cheering fans waved signs saying things like "Real Refs Rock." Players and coaches hugged the crew before kickoff.

NFL Network television announcer Rich Eisen called it "the first time ever in any sport at any level that a crowd will give a standing ovation to a referee."

Some commentators pointed out that the replacement officials did a pretty good job, despite some highly visible mistakes. Others said they simply didn't have the experience or the skill of officials who have been pushing themselves for years to get better.

"We look forward to having the finest officials in sports back on the field," NFL commissioner Roger Goodell said in a press release. "Now it's time to put the focus back on the teams and players, where it belongs." The officials agreed.

BASKETBALL

Winter is the traditional basketball season, but it's an indoor sport, so it's played year-round in a lot of places. There are also outdoor courts for play in the warm months—both organized games and pickup games. That means there are lots of places to get started and to get practice as a referee.

YOUTH AND RECREATION LEAGUES

Basketball officials who are just starting out can check with local youth and adult recreation leagues or the nearest local YMCA. The Amateur Athletic Union (AAU) sponsors sports for about half a million participants of all ages across the country and is known for its basketball

The Amateur Athletic Union sponsors sports for half a million participants. The AAU is especially known for its basketball programs.

programs. Officials need to become a member of the AAU and pay a small fee.

HIGH SCHOOL

High school officials must register and be licensed by their state interscholastic organization. In most states you must belong to a recognized officials' association. There's usually a rules exam, a background check, and a mandatory clinic or other training. There may also be a probationary period for new officials.

COLLEGE

A local community or city college is usually the next stop for officials who have high school experience. Go to a ball game and ask an official how the system works in your area. He or she can probably put you in touch with the local officials' association.

Division I NCAA conferences offer the best-paid and highest-profile jobs in college basketball, but it can take years to move up to that level. Newcomers start out in Division II or Division III conferences and work their way

The NCAA is known for its high-profile college sports, but smaller schools in the NAIA also have lots of opportunities for officials.

up. The conferences of smaller colleges in the NAIA also have great men's and women's basketball programs and a national tournament.

NBA

The National Basketball Association's Developmental League holds tryouts every year for officials who want to work in the D-League, the Women's NBA, or the NBA. It takes two years' or more experience at the high school level or higher to qualify for a tryout, and there's a fee of about $150. Want to study the rules? The NBA Rule Book and Case Book are free on the NBA Web site.

HOCKEY

Hockey officials at all levels have to be excellent skaters. They also have to be in excellent condition. While they don't have to make contact and dish it out, they do need to have endurance. Players can rest during periods. Officials can't.

MINOR HOCKEY AND AMATEUR LEAGUES

The local rink is probably the best place to start. Ask one of the officials or contact the local youth league or minor hockey association to find out about the next training seminar for beginning referees. You'll have to attend and pay a small fee to be certified. There will probably be an open-book written test as well as skating drills and instruction. There's no set age limit for hockey officials, but most leagues want their refs to be older than the players in their games.

USA Hockey is the national organization for amateur hockey in the United States. It has training and certification programs and services for officials at all levels. Beginning officials can find out about training through their local association or the USA Hockey referee-in-chief of their region. A list can be found at the USA Hockey Web site.

Most hockey leagues have no minimum age for officials, although they usually have to be older than the players. This "puck kid" in Germany has a few years to wait.

Hockey officials in both the United States and Canada are ranked according to skill and experience, and there are several levels of certification, from referees and linesmen in amateur youth leagues up to national championship play. The Hockey Canada Officiating Program has details for each level on its Web site.

HIGH SCHOOL

As with officials in other sports, high school hockey officials need to be certified by their state interscholastic association. Most associations have their information posted online, and in many states you can also take exams and get training schedules online. Officials also need to be members of their local, state, or regional associations and buy their own helmets and uniforms.

COLLEGE

The NCAA "Center Ice" Web page for arbiters has helpful information about getting certified to officiate major college hockey. The test, rulebooks, and clinics are available online. There are regional associations for college hockey officials in the United States and Canada, and most of these work as assigning organizations with colleges and conferences.

Officials who want to reach the top college level should attend as many training camps as possible, both to improve their skills and to be seen by scouts from the NHL, other pro leagues, and college programs. Be prepared for a tough workout. Scouts at this level look hard at conditioning and endurance as well as rules knowledge.

NATIONAL HOCKEY LEAGUE

Many officials reach the NHL by working their way up through the American Hockey League or the Canadian Hockey League. However the NHL also recruits in minor leagues, and it may not take as long to reach the top in

Referee Tom Peel gets ready to drop the puck at an NHL game. Many NHL officials work their way up through the American or Canadian hockey leagues.

hockey as it does in other sports. On the other hand, hockey officials' careers are usually shorter than those in other sports because it's so tough physically.

SOCCER

Soccer has the most unified training program for officials of any major sport in America. There are nearly 150,000 soccer officials at all levels in the United States.

AMATEUR AND YOUTH LEAGUES

The U.S. Soccer Federation has an extensive program for training and certification for officials at all levels. Its Web site explains what you have to do not only to become an official, but an instructor of officials, an assignor of games, and a qualified assessor of officials.

HIGH SCHOOL

There are a lot of training opportunities and game opportunities for officials in school-sponsored soccer. To work, you'll have to follow the procedures for all other sports officials in your state. Check with your state's interscholastic association to see the requirements.

COLLEGE

As in other sports, college soccer officials are trained and assigned to games by individual schools, conferences, or their officials' associations. The main officials' association is NISOA, the National Intercollegiate Soccer Officials Association.

MLS

Major League Soccer (MLS) and the U.S. Soccer Federation teamed up a few years ago to create an integrated program for training and certifying officials. In theory, all you have to do is sign up, be certified, and start working your way up the ladder. You can be qualified not only for professional matches in America but also for international FIFA (International Federation of Association Football) matches. You'll be graded all the way up the line, and you'll have to take courses and pass field tests to move up. How much you earn depends on experience and excellence.

ASSOCIATIONS, ORGANIZATIONS, AND TRAINING PROGRAMS

The following is a list of state associations that train and certify officials for high school sports. Contact your association for information on training and requirements in your state.

Alabama High School
Athletic Association
P.O. Box 242367
7325 Halcyon Summit
Drive
Montgomery, AL
36124-2367
(334) 263-6994
Web site: http://www
.ahsaa.com

Alaska School Activities
Association
4048 Laurel Street, Suite 203
Anchorage, AK 99508
(907) 563-3723
Web site: http://www.asaa
.org

Arizona Interscholastic
Association
7007 N 18th Street
Phoenix, AZ 85020-5552

(602) 385-3810
Web site: http://www
.aiaonline.org

Arkansas Activities
Association
3920 Richards Road
North Little Rock, AR
72117-2920
(501) 955-2500
Web site: http://www
.ahsaa.org

California Interscholastic
Federation
4658 Duckhorn Drive
Sacramento, CA 95834
(916) 239-4477
Web site: http://www
.cifstate.org

Colorado High School
Activities Association

14855 East Second Avenue
Aurora, CO 80011-8900
(303) 344-5050
Web site: http://www
.chsaa.org

Connecticut
Interscholastic Athletic
Conference
30 Realty Drive
Cheshire, CT 06410-1655
(203) 250-1111
Web site: http://www
.casciac.org

Delaware Interscholastic
Athletic Association
35 Commerce Way, Suite 1
Dover, DE 19904
(302) 857-3365
Web site: http://www
.doe.state.de.us/
PROGRAMS/diaa

District of Columbia
Public Schools—IAA
Department of Athletics
Hamilton School
1401 Brentwood Parkway
NE
Washington, DC
20002-2220
(202) 729-3288
Web site: http://dc.gov
/dcps

Florida High School
Athletic Association,
Inc.
1801 NW 80th Boulevard
Gainesville, FL 32606-9176
(352) 372-9551
Web site: http://www
.fhsaa.org

Georgia High School
Association
151 South Bethel Street
Thomaston, GA
30286-4187
(706) 647-7473
Web site: http://www
.ghsa.net

Hawaii High School
Athletic Association
P.O. Box 62029
1202 Prospect Street
Honolulu, HI 96839-2029
(808) 587-4495
Web site: http://www
.sportshigh.com

Idaho High School
Activities Association
P.O. Box 4667
8011 Ustick Road
Boise, ID 83704-8101
(208) 375-7027
Web site: http://www
.idhsaa.org

Illinois High School
Association
2715 McGraw Drive
Bloomington, IL 61704
(309) 663-6377
Web site: http://www
.ihsa.org

Indiana High School
Athletic Association
P.O. Box 40650
Indianapolis, IN
46240-0650
(317) 846-6601
Web site: http://www
.ihsaa.org

Iowa High School Athletic
Association
P.O. Box 10
1605 South Story Street
Boone, IA 50036-5226
(515) 432-2011
Web site: http://www
.iahsaa.org

Kansas State High School
Activities Association
P.O. Box 495
Topeka, KS 66615-1234
(785) 273-5329
Web site: http://www
.kshsaa.org

Kentucky High School
Athletic Association
2280 Executive Drive
Lexington, KY 40505-4808
(859) 299-5472
Web site: http://www
.khsaa.org

Louisiana High School
Athletic Association
12720 Old Hammond
Highway
Baton Rouge, LA 70816
(225) 296-5882
Web site: http://www
.lhsaa.org

Maine Principals'
Association
P.O. Box 2468
50 Industrial Drive
Augusta, ME 04338-2468
(207) 622-0217
Web site: http://www.mpa.cc

Maryland Public
Secondary Schools
Athletic Association
200 West Baltimore Street
Baltimore, MD 21201-1595
(410) 767-0376
Web site: http://www.
mpssaa.org

Massachusetts
Interscholastic Athletic
Association
33 Forge Parkway
Franklin, MA 02038-3135
(508) 541-7997
Web site: http://www
.miaa.net

Michigan High School
Athletic Association
1661 Ramblewood Drive
East Lansing, MI
48823-7392
(517) 332-5044
Web site: http://www
.mhsaa.com

Minnesota State High
School League
2100 Freeway Boulevard
Brooklyn Center, MN
55430-173
(763) 560-2262
Web site: http://www
.mshsl.org

Mississippi High School
Activities Association
P.O. Box 127
1201 Clinton-Raymond
Road
Clinton, MS 39060-0244

(601) 924-6400
Web site: http://www
.misshsaa.com

Missouri State High School
Activities Association
1 North Keene Street
Columbia, MO
65201-6645
(573) 875-4880
Web site: http://www
.mshsaa.org

Montana High School
Association
1 South Dakota Avenue
Helena, MT 59601-5198
(406) 442-6010
Web site: http://www
.mhsa.org

Nebraska School Activities
Association
P.O. Box 85448
Lincoln, NE 68501
(402) 489-0386
Web site: http://www
.nsaahome.org

Nevada Interscholastic
Activities Association
549 Court Street
Reno, NV 89501

(775) 453-1012
Web site: http://www
.niaa.com

New Hampshire
Interscholastic Athletic
Association
251 Clinton Street
Concord, NH 03301-8432
(603) 228-8671
Web site: http://www
.nhiaa.org

New Jersey State
Interscholastic Athletic
Association
P.O. Box 487
Robbinsville, NJ 08691-1104
(609) 259-2776
Web site: http://www
.njsiaa.org

New Mexico Activities
Association
6600 Palomas Avenue NE
Albuquerque, NM
87109-5639
(505) 923-3110
Web site: http://www.
nmact.org

New York State Public
High School Athletic
Association
8 Airport Park Boulevard

Latham, NY 12110
(518) 690-0771
Web site: http://www
.nysphsaa.org

North Carolina High School
Athletic Association
P.O. Box 3216
222 Finley Golf Course
Road
Chapel Hill, NC 27515-3216
(919) 240-7401
Web site: http://www
.nchsaa.org

North Dakota High School
Activities Association
P.O. Box 817
Valley City, ND
58072-3047
(701) 845-3953
Web site: http://www.ndh-
saa.com

Ohio High School Athletic
Association
4080 Roselea Place
Columbus, OH 43214-3069
(614) 267-2502
Web site: http://www
.ohsaa.org

Oklahoma Secondary
School Activities
Association

P.O. Box 14590
Oklahoma City, OK
    73113-0590
(405) 840-1116
Web site: http://www
    .ossaa.com

Oregon School Activities
    Association
25200 Southwest Parkway
    Avenue, Suite 1
Wilsonville, OR
    97070-9616
(503) 682-6722
Web site: http://www
    .osaa.org

Pennsylvania Interscholastic
    Athletic Association
P.O. Box 2008
Mechanicsburg, PA
    17055-0708
(717) 697-0374
Web site: http://www
    .piaa.org

Rhode Island Interscholastic
    League, Inc.
Building 6, Rhode Island
    College Campus
600 Mt. Pleasant Avenue
Providence, RI 02908-1991
(401) 272-9844
Web site: http://www
    .riil.org

South Carolina High
    School League
P.O. Box 211575
Columbia, SC
    29210-6575
(803) 798-0120
Web site: http://www
    .schsl.org

South Dakota High School
    Activities Association
804 North Euclid Avenue,
    Suite 102
Pierre, SD 57501-1217
(605) 224-9261
Web site: http://www
    .sdhsaa.com

Tennessee Secondary
    School Athletic
    Association
3333 Lebanon Road
Hermitage, TN
    37076-2003
(615) 889-6740
Web site: http://www
    .tssaa.org

Texas University
    Interscholastic League
1701 Manor Road
Austin, TX 78722
(512) 471-5883
Web site: http://www
    .uiltexas.org

Utah High School
   Activities Association
199 East 7200 South
Midvale, UT 84047-1534
(801) 566-0681
Web site: http://www
   .uhsaa.org

Vermont Principals
   Association
Two Prospect Street, Suite 3
Montpelier, VT 05602
(802) 229-0547
Web site: http://www
   .vpaonline.org

Virginia High School League
1642 State Farm Boulevard
Charlottesville, VA
   22911-8609
(434) 977-8475
Web site: http://www
   .vhsl.org

Washington Interscholastic
   Activities Association
435 Main Avenue South
Renton, WA 98057
(425) 687-8585
Web site: http://www
   .wiaa.com

West Virginia Secondary
   School Activities
   Commission

2875 Staunton Turnpike
Parkersburg, WV
   26104-7219
(304) 485-5494
Web site: http://www
   .wvssac.org

Wisconsin Interscholastic
   Athletic Association
5516 Vern Holmes Drive
Stevens Point, WI
   54482-8833
(715) 344-8580
Web site: http://www
   .wiaawi.org

Wyoming High School
   Activities Association
731 East 2nd Street
Casper, WY 82601-2620
(307) 577-0614
Web site: http://www
   .whsaa.org

BASEBALL UMPIRE SCHOOLS

Harry Wendelstedt Umpire
   School
Administrative Office
P.O. Box 1079
Albion, MI 49224
(386) 672-4879
Web site: http://www
   .umpireschool.com

Jim Evans Academy of
Professional Umpiring
200 South Wilcox Street,
#508
Castle Rock, CO 80104
(303) 290-7411
Web site: http://www
.umpireacademy.com

Major League Baseball
Umpire Camp
245 Park Avenue
New York, NY 10167
(212) 931-7537
Web site: http://www
.mlbuc.com

The Umpire School
P.O. Box A
St. Petersburg, FL
33731-1950
(877) 799-8677
Web site: http://www
.therightcall.net

MAJOR SPORTS ASSOCIATIONS AND ORGANIZATIONS

Amateur Baseball Umpires
Association
200 South Wilcox Street,
#508

Castle Rock, CO 80104
(303) 290-7411
Web site: http://www
.umpire.org

American Alliance for
Health, Physical
Education, Recreation
and Dance
1900 Association Drive
Reston, VA 20191-1598
(703) 476-3400; (800)
213-7193
Web site: http://www
.aahperd.org

American Youth Soccer
Organization (AYSO)
AYSO National Office
19750 South Vermont
Avenue, Suite 200
Torrance, CA 90502
USA-AYSO (800-872-2976)
Web site: http://www
.AYSO.org

Arena Football League
75 East Wacker, #400
Chicago, IL 60601
(312) 332-5510
Web site: http://www
.arenafootball.com

Babe Ruth League, Inc.
P.O. Box 5000

Trenton, NJ 08638
(609) 695-1434
Web site: http://www
.baberuthleague.org

International Association
of Approved Basketball
Officials
P.O. Box 355
Carlisle, PA 17013-035
(717) 713-8129
Web site: http://www
.iaabo.org/contact
_us.htm

Little League Baseball, Inc.
539 U.S. 15
Williamsport, PA 17702
(570) 326-1921
Web site: http://www
.littleleague.org

National Alliance for
Youth Sports (NAYS)
2050 Vista Parkway
West Palm Beach, FL
33411
(800) 688-KIDS (5437)
Web site: http://www
.nays.org

National Association
of Intercollegiate
Athletics (NAIA)
1200 Grand Boulevard

Kansas City, MO 64106
(816) 595-8180
Web site: http: //www
.NAIA.org

National Association of
Sports Officials
2017 Lathrop Avenue
Racine, WI 53405
(262) 632-5448
Web site: http://http://www
.naso.org

National Basketball
Association (NBA)
645 5th Avenue
New York, NY 10022
(212) 407-8000
Web site: http://www
.NBA.org

National Collegiate Athletic
Association (NCAA)
P.O. Box 6222
Indianapolis, Indiana
46206-6222
(317) 917-6222
Web site: http://www
.NCAA.org

National Federation of
State High School
Associations (NFHS)
P.O. Box 690
Indianapolis, IN 46206

(317) 972.6900
Web site: http://www
.NFHS.org

National Football League
(NFL)
280 Park Avenue
New York, NY 10017
(212) 450-2000
Web site: http://www
.NFL.org

National Junior College
Athletic Association
(NJCAA)
1631 Mesa Avenue, Suite B
Colorado Springs, CO
80906
(719) 590-9788
Web site: http://www
.njcaa.org

Pony Baseball and Softball
P.O. Box 225
Washington, PA 15301
(724) 225-1060
Web site: http://www
.pony.org

Pop Warner Football
Pop Warner Little
Scholars, Inc.
586 Middletown
Boulevard, Suite C-100
Langhorne, PA 19047

(215) 752-2691
Web site: http://www
.popwarner.com

Soccer Association For
Youth (SAY)
Enterprise Business Park
2812 East Kemper Road
Cincinnati, OH 45241
(800) 233-7291; (513)
769-3800
Web site: http://www
.SAYSOCCER.org

Soccer in the Streets (SITS)
3845 Green Industrial Way
Atlanta, GA 30341
(888) 436-5833
E-mail: info@soccerstreets
.org

USA Football
45 North Pennsylvania
Street, Suite 700
Indianapolis, IN 46204
(877) 536-6822
Web site: http://www
.usafootball.com/
game-officials

USA Hockey
1775 Bob Johnson Drive
Colorado Springs, CO
80906-4090
(719) 576-USAH (8724)

Web site: http://www.
USAHOCKEY.com

USA Volleyball
4065 Sinton Road, Suite 200
Colorado Springs, CO
80907
(719) 228-6800
Web site: http://www
.teamusa.org

USA Volleyball Beach
Headquarters
200 Pier Avenue, Suite 134
Hermosa Beach, CA 90254
(310) 975-3930
Web site: http://www
.teamUSA.org

United States Olympic
Committee
One Olympic Plaza
Colorado Springs, CO
80909
(719) 632-5551
Web site: http://www
.teamusa.org

United States Soccer
Federation
1801-1811 South Prairie
Avenue
Chicago, IL 60616
(312) 808-1300

Web site: http://www
.ussoccer.com

Women's National
Basketball Association
645 5th Avenue
New York, NY 10022
(212) 407-8000
Web site: http://www
.wnba.com

A CAREER IN SPORTS OFFICIATING AT A GLANCE

REFEREES AND UMPIRES

ACADEMICS

- High school diploma at most levels of sport

EXPERIENCE

- Volunteer opportunities to start in youth and recreation leagues

CAREER PATHS

- Officials may move up to high school sports, college sports, and professional sports

DUTIES AND RESPONSIBILITIES

- Officiate sporting events and enforce the rules of the game
- Promote safety
- Ensure fairness
- Encourage player development
- Promote good sportsmanship

UMPIRES, REFEREES, AND OTHER SPORTS OFFICIALS

SIGNIFICANT POINTS

- The job is highly stressful.

- Officials must make split-second decisions, and their calls are often disputed.

- Work is seasonal and a part-time job for most officials.

- The job often requires extensive travel.

- There are no educational requirements for most beginning officials.

- A high school diploma is required for most school and professional officials.

NATURE OF THE WORK

Referees and umpires officiate sporting events, enforce the rules of the game, and assess penalties when necessary.

They inspect sports equipment and examine all participants to ensure safety and signal participants to begin and stop play.

TRAINING

Athletic associations, conferences, leagues, and officials' associations arrange training camps, clinics, and seminars for officials in off-seasons. There are several permanent schools for baseball umpires. Some sports such as soccer have nationwide training programs. Many sports officials learn on the job by volunteering to officiate youth and recreation league games, practices, and scrimmages.

OTHER QUALIFICATIONS

Officials must be in good physical condition. They must be fair-minded, patient, and open to informed criticism. They must also be able to tolerate fans who are sometimes abusive.

ADVANCEMENT

Officials usually begin work as volunteers in youth sports and try to work their way up to high school and college sports. A few advance to professional sports.

JOB OUTLOOK

Employment of umpires, referees, and other sports officials is expected to increase 20 percent from 2010 to 2020, faster than the average for all occupations. Most new jobs are expected to be in high school sports and in women's sports at the college level.

WORK ENVIRONMENT

Officials work in parks and sports stadiums. In some sports, they work in teams, but at some levels there may be only one official at a game.

GLOSSARY

anonymous Not identified; not known by name.

arbitrator An impartial person who is appointed to settle a dispute.

baseline The line that marks the end of a basketball or volleyball court.

certify License; approve; confirm that something or someone is valid.

clinic An instruction course on a particular subject.

conference A group of sports teams that play each other.

conflict A struggle or disagreement between two or more parties.

credibility Believability; trustworthiness; the ability to make people trust and believe.

decisive Able to make quick and sure decisions.

dedication Commitment to something such as a job or purpose.

enhance Increase; improve.

execute Carry out.

impart Give; pass on something such as knowledge.

integrity Honesty; the quality of having strong morals.

interscholastic Among different schools.

intimidate Scare or bully someone into doing something.

motivation A desire to do something.

neural Related to the nervous system.

official Publicly recognized and trusted; being taken as authority.

presence An impressive appearance.

preventive Designed to keep something bad from happening.

probationary Being tried out for approval.

procedure An established, official way to do something.

profession A paid job that requires training and qualification.

prowess Skill in doing an activity.

requirement Something that is necessary; something that must be done to accomplish something else.

rigorous Strict; thorough and accurate.

scrutinize Look closely; inspect.

technique A way of doing something, usually something that takes practice.

tirade A long, angry rant.

trait A distinguishing feature.

unimposing Small and meek; not aggressive looking.

verbal Related to words.

visualize Form a mental image of something; imagine.

Amateur Baseball Umpires Association (ABUA)
200 South Wilcox Street, #508
Castle Rock, CO 80104
(303) 290-7411
Web site: http://www.umpire.org
The ABUA is a national organization for umpires in youth league, high school, and college baseball. It conducts teaching programs and provides insurance for members.

Canadian Interuniversity Sport (CIS)
801 King Edward, Suite N205
Ottawa, ON K1N 6N5
Canada
(613) 562-5670
Web site: http://english.cis-sic.ca
CIS is the national organization for twelve major college sports in Canada. It oversees competition leading to national championships and honors student athletes.

International Association of Approved Basketball Officials (IAABO)
P.O. Box 355
Carlisle, PA 17013-035
(717) 713-8129
Web site: http://www.iaabo.org/contact_us.htm
The IAABO has local boards in thirty-eight states and eleven countries. It offers training programs on rules, mechanics, and techniques of officiating, and on organization of local officials' groups.

Little League Baseball
539 US Route 15 Highway
P.O. Box 3485
Williamsport, PA 17701-0485
(570) 326-1921
Web site: http://www.littleleague.org
Little League Baseball is the best-known program in the
United States and abroad for young baseball and softball
players. Its Web site has information on umpire clinics
and schools as well as how to register, how to be certified, and other information.

National Association of Sports Officials (NASO)
2017 Lathrop Avenue
Racine, WI 53405
(262) 632-5448
Web site: http://www.naso.org
The NASO has nearly nineteen thousand members. It
provides training materials, education, and benefits,
including insurance.

National Federation of State High School Associations (NFHS)
P.O. Box 690
Indianapolis, IN 46206
(317) 972-6900
Web site: https://nfhs.arbitersports.com
The NFHS publishes playing rules in sixteen sports for boys
and girls. It provides insurance and other services for
officials through the NFHS officials' organization.

Referee
2017 Lathrop Avenue
Racine, WI 53405
(800) 733-6100

Web site: http://www.referee.com

Referee is a national magazine for officials in all sports, and officials write much of its content. It is affiliated with NASO and also publishes training materials and sells officials' uniforms and apparel.

Sports Officials Canada (SOC)
6927 Bilberry Drive
Ottawa, ON K1C 2C1
Canada
(613) 837-7298
Web site: http://www.sportsofficials.ca

SOC is an advocacy group representing officials at all levels of sport. It promotes excellence in officiating, arranges for insurance coverage, and holds an annual conference.

United States Soccer Federation (USSF)
1801-1811 South Prairie Avenue
Chicago, IL 60616
(312) 808-1300
Web site: http://www.ussoccer.com

The USSF is the national organization for soccer in the United States. It has training programs and other services for officials at all levels of the sport.

USA Football
45 North Pennsylvania Street, Suite 700
Indianapolis, IN 46204
(877) 536-6822
Web site: http://www2.usafootball.com

USA Football is a membership organization that provides education, certification, insurance, and other services for officials. Many of its resources are available to members online.

USA Hockey
1175 Bob Johnson Drive
Colorado Springs, CO 80906-4090
(719) 576-8724
Web site: http://www.usahockey.com
USA Hockey is the governing body for the sport in the
United States. It conducts clinics and produces training
manuals and videos through its Officiating Education
Program.

USA Volleyball
4065 Sinton Road, Suite 200
Colorado Springs, CO 80907
(719) 228-6800
Web site: http://www.teamusa.org
USA Volleyball is the governing body for the sport in the
United States. It has clinics and certifies officials for
indoor, junior, and beach volleyball. It also offers training material, officiating opportunities, rules, and other
information on its Web site.

WEB SITES

Due to the changing nature of Internet links, Rosen
Publishing has developed an online list of Web sites related
to the subject of this book. This site is updated regularly.
Please use this link to access the list:

http://www.rosenlinks.com/GCSI/Ref

FOR FURTHER READING

American Sport Education Program. *Successful Sports Officiating*. Champaign, IL: Human Kinetics, 2011.

Burleson, Dick. *You Better Be Right: My 25 Years as an SEC Football Official*. Ipswich, MA: Ebsco Media, 2006.

Caminsky, Jeffrey. *The Referee's Survival Guide*. Livonia, MI: New Alexandria Press, 2007.

Capeloto, Glenn. *You're in the Front Row: How to Kick Off Your Career in Sports Even If You're Not a Star Athlete*. Tempe, AZ: Facts on Demand Press, 2012.

Cashion, Red. *First Dooowwwnnn...and Life to Go! How an Enthusiastic Approach Changed Everything for the Most Colorful Referee in NFL History*. Bloomington, IN: AuthorHouse, 2012.

Colgate, Bob, ed. 2013 *NFHS High School Football: Rules by Topic*. Indianapolis, IN: National Federation of State High School Associations, 2013.

Donaghy, Tim. *Personal Foul: A First-Person Account of the Scandal That Rocked the NBA*. Tampa Bay, FL: VTi-Group, 2009.

Easley, Lance. *Making the Call: Living with Your Decisions*. Uhrichsville, OH: Barbour Books, 2013.

Ferguson. *Careers in Focus: Sports*. 4th ed. New York, NY: Infobase Publishing, 2008.

Hoffman, Shirl J. *Careers in Sport, Fitness, and Exercise: The Authoritative Guide for Landing the Job of Your Dreams*. Champaign, IL: Human Kinetics, 2011.

Hofstetter, Adam B. *Cool Careers Without College for People Who Love Sports*. New York, NY: Rosen Publishing Group, 2007.

Hopkins, Elliot B., ed. *NFHS 2013 High School Baseball Rules by Topic: Rules, Caseplays Rationales Linked.* Indianapolis, IN: National Federation of State High School Associations, 2013.

Liner, Mike. *It's Not All Black and White: From Junior High to the Sugar Bowl, an Inside Look at Football Through the Eyes of an Official.* New York, NY: Skyhorse Publishing, 2009.

Markbreit, Jerry, and Alan Steinberg. *Last Call: Memoirs of an NFL Referee.* New York, NY: Sports Publishing, 2001.

Meltzer, Peter E. *So You Think You Know Baseball? A Fan's Guide to the Official Rules.* New York, NY: W.W. Norton & Company, 2013.

Phillips, Dave, and Rob Rains. *Center Field on Fire: An Umpire's Life with Pine Tar Bats, Spitballs, and Corked Personalities.* Chicago, IL: Triumph Books, 2004.

Stern, Jeffrey. *Football Game Intelligence: The Difference-Maker in Officiating.* Racine, WI: Referee Enterprises, Inc., and the National Association of Sports Officials, 2011.

Stern, Jeffrey. *Football Officiating Mechanics Illustrated: Four and Five Person High School Crews.* Racine, WI: Referee Training Center, 2013.

Stern, Jeffrey. *High School Football Penalty Enforcements Made Easy.* Racine, WI: Referee Enterprises, 2009.

Stern, Jeffrey. *The Ultimate Book on Holding.* Racine, WI: Referee Enterprises, Inc., and the National Association of Sports Officials, 2010.

Triumph Books. 2013 *Official Rules of Major League Baseball.* Chicago, IL: Triumph Books, 2013.

Turkington, Carol A., and Alecia T. Devantier. *Extraordinary Jobs in Sports.* New York, NY: Infobase Publishing, 2007.

Vogt, Randy. *Preventive Officiating: How a Referee Avoids Trouble on the Soccer Field.* Seattle, WA: CreateSpace Independent Publishing Platform, 2010.

Wargo, John M. *What Now?: The Essential Guide for New Soccer Referees*. Seattle, WA: BookSurge Publishing, 2007.

Weber, Bruce. *As They See 'Em: A Fan's Travels in the Land of Umpires*. New York, NY: Scribner, 2009.

Wicks, Ron. *A Referee's Life*. Renfrew, ON: General Store Publishing House, 2012.

Wynns, Theresia, ed. *2012–13 NFHS High School Basketball Rules Simplified & Illustrated*. Indianapolis, IN: National Federation of State High School Associations, 2013.

Yearout, Rick. *Could You Be the Referee? A Compilation of Football Referee's Signals*. Bloomington, IN: AuthorHouse, 2008.

BIBLIOGRAPHY

Borden, Sam. "For Two-Way Referee, It's N.F.L. One Day, College Basketball the Next." *New York Times*, March 13, 2012. Retrieved August 20, 2013 (http://www.nytimes.com/2012/03/14/sports/for-two-way-referee-its-nfl-one-day-college-basketball-the-next.html?pagewanted=all&_r=1&).

Clary, Jack. *Careers in Sports*. Chicago, IL: Contemporary Books, Inc., 1982.

Demetriou, George, and Bill Topp. *Smart Baseball Umpiring: How to Get Better Every Game*. Franksville, WI: Referee Enterprises Inc., 1998.

Dixon, Oscar. "Barkley's Race with 67-Year-Old Ref Steals Show on All-Star Saturday." *USA Today*, February 19, 2007. Retrieved Aug. 7, 2013 (http://usatoday30.usatoday.com/sports/basketball/allstar/2007-02-17-saturday-competitions_x.htm).

Dubois, Muriel L. *I Like Sports: What Can I Be?* Mankato, MN: Capstone Press, 2001.

Field, Shelly. *Career Opportunities in the Sports Industry*. New York, NY: Ferguson, 2010.

Grunska, Jerry, ed. *Successful Sports Officiating*. Champaign, IL: Human Kinetics, 1999.

Heitzmann, William Ray. *Careers for Sports Nuts & Other Athletic Types*. Lincolnwood, IL: VGM Career Horizons, 1997.

Hood, Bruce. *Calling the Shots: Memoirs of an NHL Referee*. Toronto, ON, Canada: Stoddart Publishing Co. Ltd., 1988.

Menard, Valerie. *Latinos at Work Careers in Sports*. Bear, DE: Mitchell Lane Publishers, 2002.

National Association of Sports Officials. "A Covenant with
Sports Officials." NASO. Retrieved August 21, 2013
(http://www.naso.org/Resources/Covenant.aspx).

National Youth Sports Officials Association. *101 Tips
for Youth Sports Officials*. Franksville, WI: Referee
Enterprises Inc., 1997.

Pasternak, Ceel, and Linda Thornburg. *Cool Careers for Girls
in Sports*. Manassas Park, VA: Impact Publications, 1999.

Powers, Richie, with Mark Mulvoy. *Overtime! An
Uninhibited Account of a Referee's Life in the NBA*. New
York, NY: David McKay Co., 1975.

Reeves, Diane Lindsey. *Career Ideas for Kids Who Like
Sports*. New York, NY: Checkmark Books, Inc., 1998.

Roberts, Robin. *Careers for Women Who Love Sports*.
Brookfield, CT: Millbrook Press, Inc., 2000.

San Francisco Soccer Referee Association. "Author's
Biography Robert Evans Ph.D." SFSRA. Retrieved
August 18, 2013 (http://www.sfsra.org/main/shopping).

Schachter, Norman. *Close Calls: The Confessions of a NFL
Referee*. New York, NY: William Morrow and Co., 1981.

Zillgitt, Jeff. "For NFL Officials, Scrutiny Begins Long
Before Kickoff." *USA Today*, October 10, 2007. Retrieved
August 22, 2013 (http://usatoday30.usatoday.com/
sports/football/nfl/2007-10-09-officials_N.htm).

INDEX

E

Evans, Billy, 49
Evans, Robert, 74–75

F

fairness, 11, 13–16
fighting, 59–60
fitness, 14, 42–43, 55, 111
flowing blood rules, 12–13
football referees, career overview,
    11–12
  college, 86–87
  high school, 86
  National Football League, 87,
  youth and recreation leagues, 86

H

Harvey, Doug, 50
high school sports
  officiating, 22, 24–25, 82, 90,
    94, 96
  organizations that offer train-
    ing programs, 98–105
Hochuli, Ed, 40–41, 43
hockey referees, career overview, 11
  college, 94–95
  high school, 94
  minor hockey and amateur
    leagues, 92–94
  National Hockey League, 95–96
Holland, Time, 31
Hubbard, Cal, 50

I

independent contractors, 64–65,
  70–73
Intercollegiate Tennis Association, 23
International Federation of Association Football, 75, 97
International Tennis Federation, 23

K

Kantner, Dee, 30
Klem, Bill, 50

L

liability insurance, 65, 69, 71, 73
Little League, 7, 30, 33, 47, 81–
  82, 106

M

Major League Baseball, 27, 29,
  39, 83
Major League Soccer, 40, 97
major sports organizations that
  offer training for, 62–63,
  105–108
McGowan, Bill, 50–51
mechanics of sports, 13, 33–34, 47
medical insurance, 71, 73
mental toughness, 7, 15, 51–55,
  59, 61–62

ABOUT THE AUTHOR

Larry Gerber is a former Associated Press journalist who has covered Olympic Games, World University Games, cycling, baseball, basketball, football, and other sports. He played Little League baseball and high school basketball. Gerber lives in Los Angeles.

PHOTO CREDITS

Cover, p. 1 (referee) © iStockphoto.com/dstephens; cover, p. 1 (field) © iStockphoto.com/dehooks; pp. 4–5 Maxisport/Shutterstock.com; pp. 6, 48, 50, 62, 66, 76 © AP Images; p. 10 NFL Photos/AP Images; p. 12 Stuart Franklin/Bongarts/Getty Images; pp. 14–15 Bob Thomas/Popperfoto/Getty Images; p. 17 Anderson Ross/Digital Vision/Getty Images; pp. 20–21 Steven King/Icon SMI; p. 23 Mike Hewitt/Getty Images; p. 24 Visions of America/Universal Images Group/Getty Images; p. 26 Jonathan Daniel/Getty Images; p. 29 Charlotte Observer/McClatchy-Tribune/Getty Images; p. 32 Aspen Photo/Shutterstock.com; pp. 36–37 The Elkhart Truth, Jennifer Shephard/AP Images; pp. 38–39 Dave Sanford/National Hockey League/Getty Images; pp. 40–41 Bill Frakes/Sports Illustrated/Getty Images; p. 43 Jed Jacobsohn/Getty Images; p. 52 Claus Andersen/Getty Images; p. 54 Matthew Brown/E+/Getty Images; p. 56 skynesher/Vetta/Getty Images; p. 60 Francois Lacasse/National Hockey League/Getty Images; p. 71 Al Messerschmidt/Getty Images; p. 72 Mitchell Layton/Getty Images; p. 80 Todd Rosenberg/Sports Illustrated/Getty Images; pp. 83, 84 Al Bello/Getty Images; p. 90 Sacramento Bee/Randall Benton/ZUMA Press; p. 91 The Chronicle-Tribune/Jeff Morehead/AP Images; p. 93 Friedemann Vogel/Bongarts/Getty Images; p. 95 Len Redkoles/National Hockey League/Getty Images; interior design elements (graph) © iStockphoto.com/hudiemm, (stripes) Lost & Taken; pp. 9, 28, 47, 64, 79, 98, 109, 110, 113, 115, 119, 122, 124 © iStockphoto.com unless otherwise noted. From top left ultramarinfoto, Kayann, VIPDesignUSA, plherrera, cb34inc, yail12, Jimmy Anderson, dbrskinner, dswebb, Gannet77, Sergieiev/Shutterstock.com, gzaleckas, choja, cscredon, peepo.

Designer: Nicole Russo; Editor: Shalini Saxena;
Photo Researcher: Karen Huang